The
CAREER
PLANNING
GUIDE

FIND THE CAREER YOU DESERVE · IN 10 SHORT CHAPTERS

PLANNING ADULTING

KYLE
CRANDALL

Cover designed by 360 Graphics Design Firm.

Kyle Crandall
www.PlanningAdulting.com

Printed in the United States of America

First Printing: May 2019
Kindle Direct Publishing

ISBN- 9781096555711

Dedicated to my wife and our awesome life together.

CONTENTS

PREQUEL

WHY YOU SHOULD BUY *THIS BOOK

*THERE ARE MANY LIKE IT, BUT THIS ONE IS YOURS

The purpose for this guide is to inspire. Not for me to inspire you, but for you to inspire yourself. To find a direction to head towards, and the motivation to do so. By the end of this quest it is my goal for you to have a clear understanding of what career you want during your pursuit of happiness.

You may be a high school student, college student, or already in the work force. You may have children, responsibilities, and maybe even reasons you are telling yourself you cannot make a change to find the career you deserve to have. This is not the case. We all have options – sometimes it's the vast sea of options we have that can debilitate us from deciding a direction to go. Fear not, we're going to "weigh" these options on the scale of life.

You may be standing at the bookstore, reading the first few pages, deciding if this is worth whatever price it has stamped on it. I am proof that this guide works, and the time taken to follow this stepping-stone is worth every second. It is not my intention to put you inside my strange head, but to help you use my research and planning skills in your own mind to find your own North Star.

So, who am I? Some "young buck" from New York trying to give everybody advice? Negative ghost rider. Definitely not. I have done well, but I'm not the type of person to flaunt it (intentionally at least) or enjoy talking about it. I am extremely grateful for what I have and may be the happiest person alive. One of my goals is to help others rise to their potential –by helping them find what direction that potential may be best pointed.

I simply want to show you how I bought my first investment house and $20,000 motorhome at 22 and finished my bachelor's at 23 while Active Duty in the Marine Corps. How I became my franchises' youngest franchisee *ever* at 24, bought my second house, first commercial property, started two more businesses and wrote this guide at 25.

Ok. Started writing this guide at 25. I am now 31, with a beautiful wife, three houses (two investments, others sold in the past), a huge awesome barn/office, multiple businesses and two more major ones in the works. I've traveled through 45ish U.S. States, Greece, Switzerland (twice), Germany (Oktoberfest), Austria, Liechtenstein, half of the Caribbean and a few Mexico destinations, etc. I drive very custom vehicles, have multiple "toys" and haven't worried about spending a dollar, or a thousand dollars since my own time of career planning.

Now, do I promise you will make your first $1,000,000 before 30 and it will be easy? Nope. *Google* says 8.3% of the U.S. population are millionaires. Business owners make up 47% of these millionaires. Business owners who "make their own hours." If you call going to bed late, waking up in the middle of the night to write down and decipher ideas and forgetting to go back to bed; "making your own hours" - good for you. Not every career is for everyone, hence this guide.

If money is your direct objective, strap in; while this guide is not for becoming rich, it may help you find the career you deserve to get you there. This guide will require you to develop a goal. A vow to yourself and to spend hours of real, true, American blood, sweat and tears to complete it. Remember, I spent 6 years on and off writing this guide. Determination is going to be needed down this strange yellow brick road.

We're going to use a clear-cut, kiln dried, hog tied method to get you where you want to be, and then create a plan to make it so. Through this method I found that I wanted to be an entrepreneur. I then took the steps of market research, planning, projections, loan meetings and more for ideas from helicopter crop dusting, a local bar-restaurant, to opening a Charleston club. I'm sure there were other ideas I can't even remember and probably blocked out of my mind at this point from sheer volume. This guide will help you sift through your own ideas and organize them in my copyrighted chart.

Ok enough about me. Take this journey step by step, chapter by chapter and remove interruptions and distractions when you do so. You must take this seriously if you want it to work. Even if that means just 30 minutes per day on your lunch break, perfect. Just do it without distractions, or if you are like me you will get impatient, bored and not do it as well as you could. When an idea or thought pops in your head but it doesn't fit into the chapter you are working on, check out the table of contents again to get a grasp of where it could fit and:

WRITE IT DOWN!

NEVER DELETE SOMETHING FROM YOUR CHART. YOU WILL REGRET IT!

THIS BOOK IS THE FIRST STEP TOWARDS A MORE REWARDING LIFE

THROUGH EXERCISES AND GUIDED RELFECTION.

TAKE YOUR TIME COMPLETING THEM; NO MATTER HOW SHORT THE CHAPTER!

PREQUEL 2

A REQUIRED MINDSET

A positive mental attitude is required to effectively use this guide. It is the single most important aspect to your success that it warrants its own prequel.

"If you think in negative terms you will get negative results. If you think in positive terms you will get positive results. Believe and succeed." – Vincent Peale

---

When you use *Google* to search negativity, you will find a force so strong it can cripple empires and remove the meanings of life. When you *Google* positivity however you find more than the plus sign of a battery; you find the meanings of life. I have pinpointed my meaning of life to fulfilled happiness. Actually; if you Google those two words, there is difficulty distinguishing between them. Being happy is being fulfilled. Both belong to you, and as Americans we have been born and bred through decades of growth to only be fulfilled with happiness when our purpose includes growth to our communities – a career.

Unfortunately, America is also becoming more negative daily. This requires time and effort to notice and overcome it. The American Dream has expanded so much throughout history, our search to have absolutely everything in a sea full of possibilities has become debilitating. This dream, in the time of our parents and grandparents, was of a happy, fulfilled life of freedom.

Today the American Dream is convoluted with technology and industrialization. Gone are the days in society that goals are primarily happiness and success based, but now predominately based on objects and belongings. We Americans get too wrapped up in needing the new iPhone or a shiny new car that will be an "old body style" in just a short time. Happiness comes quicker when we are less materialistic and object oriented, but **we are born into a society of it**. It says a lot that if you *Google* "the opposite of materialistic" you will find words like divine, intellectual, ungreedy, dedicated and even unconventional.

I would love to copy and paste multiple books into this guide, but I know you wouldn't buy it if it was 10,000 pages long. What I will do is make my own "*Cliff Notes*" and give you my own personal thoughts from them.

Take into account the words of Robert F. Kennedy (brother of JFK) on satisfaction: "Too much and for too long, we seemed to have surrendered personal excellence and community values in the mere accumulation of material things. Our Gross National Product, now, is over $800 billion dollars a year, but that Gross National Product – if we judge the United States of America by that – that Gross National Product counts air pollution and cigarette advertising, and ambulances to clear our highways of carnage. It counts special locks for our doors and the jails for the people who break them. It counts the destruction of the redwood and the loss of our natural wonder in chaotic sprawl. It counts napalm and counts nuclear warheads and armored cars for the police to fight the riots in our cities. It counts Whitman's rifle and Speck's knife, and the television programs which glorify violence in order to sell toys to our children. Yet the gross national product does not allow for the health of our children, the quality of their education, or the joy of their play. It does not include the beauty of our poetry or the strength of our marriages, the intelligence of our public debate or the integrity of our public officials. It measures neither our wit nor our courage, neither our wisdom nor our learning, neither our compassion nor our devotion to our country, it measures everything in short, except that which makes life worthwhile. And it can tell us everything about America except why we are proud that we are Americans."

Ikigai

If you research the Japanese word "Ikigai" you will find an individual's reason to be. The reason why an individual gets out of bed in the morning. You can search high and low for your own Ikigai, but most sources explain that **it's usually positive and in help to others.** Yep, that explains my Ikigai; to spread positivity and help others along the way. More than just words, I strive to be a more positive, patient and helpful person every day. You could call my drive a goal, but it's more a vow to myself. Remember, *"If you think in positive terms you will get positive results. Believe and succeed".*

While considering your future remember that *"No man can enrich himself unless he enriches others"* – Earl Nightingale. Your career possibilities must provide value to others to not only receive payment for rendered services, but to gain personal satisfaction for our basic need to help others.

PREQUEL 3

MAKE A VOW

The Undefeated Mind – by Dr. Alex Lickerman

Dr. Lickerman discusses so many useful ideals in his book that can help throughout this search. To start, he says that *"Making a strong goal not only helps you stay committed to it but engenders hardiness in other aspects as well."* You're going to need a goal that not only helps you today and tomorrow but perseveres this endeavor.

A goal isn't just necessary; it's required. Dr. Lickerman states in his book that *"the more concrete and understood our goal is the more possible it will be to attain. Make specific plans to set aside a certain amount of time to focus on this project. Choose a schedule and a deadline. Do not leave it for the spare time that may come up but create the time to spend."* I say, plan the same time every day. Your lunch break, an hour right after work or school, etc. Make it repeated and consistent, make this part of your daily routine to ensure it happens.

Doctor Lickerman goes on to explain that day dreaming is expecting someone else to do something for you or waiting for some outside force to magically take control and make things happen. Making a vow to yourself puts you in the driver seat making sure you take the action necessary to find a solution and make it work. Simply wishing or dreaming of the perfect career can keep you from attaining it.

You must open your field of view and understand that something you see in one light, may be completely different in another light. You may, for example, sit at a restaurant going through a menu over and over again. You may notice you hovered over the same item multiple times and end up choosing this option, even though it may not have been the exact choice you were looking for at first. Although one meal at dinner is ok to "settle on" and a lifelong career is not, it is important to consider all possibilities that may catch our eye and further evaluate them.

"Optimism yields persistence" – Dr. Alex Lickerman

Be optimistic in your search. Do not quickly glance over a possibility and dismiss it.

"The greater that we believe we can do something, the greater the chance we will actually do it." – Dr. Alex Lickerman

---

Believe in yourself that you can find the career you deserve, and you will.

When you see this symbol, STOP and <u>contemplate the project outlined.</u>

Move only a few sentences or paragraphs at a time.

<u>DO NOT PROGRESS UNTIL YOU ARE OUT OF THOUGHTS</u> to annotate.

It is time to make a vow to yourself. A vow to find the career you deserve, a vow with substance behind it. Why do you want this career? Are you trying to overcome a current situation or position? What is the reason you are using this guide? For me, it was to become successful. Not only a person that my family (and I) could be proud of, but also success and some expendable income to go with it ☺.

No matter the reason, it is important to understand your drive so it can be reinforced.

Why do you want a career?

_____

_____

Are you trying to overcome a current situation or position?

_____

_____

Why do you have this guide?

_____

_____

If any of these reasons are for another person – what is YOUR reason?

_____

_____

Blend these answers together to find a basic, concrete goal or vow to yourself.

You are completing this guide and striving for positive change and growth because:

_____

_____

THIS IS YOUR VOW!

Hopefully you took the time to find your drive; your reason to find the career you deserve. It is important to understand why you want a career to help guide you. Now that you understand why, you've created an unbreakable vow to yourself to not give up until you find your next steps.

INTRODUCTION –

THE LAST PREQUEL & "THE CHART"

The best way to explain what must go on in your head during this endeavor is not through my own words, but through those of Earl Nightingale in *The Strangest Secret.* I jotted down my favorite quotes, but without listening to it multiple times they will not have as much substance.

 Go to *YouTube* and type in "The Strangest Secret by Earl Nightingale."
It should be just over 31 minutes, 30 seconds long.
It's old, slow at times, but worth listening to over and over again.
These are a few of my favorite quotes:

"You are what you think about." – Earl Nightingale

You can retrain your mind to change yourself. You can get yourself out of a rut, just by changing your mentality. Likewise, if you think little of yourself or tell yourself you will never be more – it will be true. You must focus on and work on your goals; not daydream about them.

You must do this every hour of every day. Whatever it takes to constantly remind yourself to think in a certain way. Finding it tough to get motivated to stay busy? Put a sticky note on your cell phone so when you look at your phone you force yourself to put thought into getting moving. Plan what you will do, how long it will last- and so on. If you train your mind in this fashion, odds are you won't want to let yourself down.

Stuck on a certain portion of this guide? Same thing! Carry a reminder around with you and look at it periodically throughout the day. You may be surprised what pops into your mind when you are grocery shopping or some other daily task. Remember – *"What's wrong with men today? Men* [and women ☺] *simply don't think"* – Earl Nightingale. Force yourself to think of the current topic you are working on throughout the day and utilize time you normally don't. You will be happily surprised with the outcome when you control your thoughts, not let them control you!

"Success is the progressive realization of a worthy ideal."
"Success is anyone who is doing a predetermined job because that is what they decided to do, deliberately; only 1/20 does this." – Earl Nightingale

Success in one's eyes may look drastically different through another's. You may jot down that you want a career to help others and maybe money has nothing to do with it – there is nothing wrong with that at all! That's great! Likewise, another person solely may want to make as much money as possible. Success to one person looks completely different to another. It is your success and happiness you are working towards. Be deliberate.

"People with goals succeed because they know where they are going." – Earl Nightingale

How many people actually end up doing exactly what they wanted to without TRYING to get there? Probably close to none. Some paths may be short and some long but knowing where the path goes is paramount. How do you get from A to B if you have no idea what B is? Have a plan.

"We become what we think about." – Earl Nightingale

I have trained my mind to complete a task even when I'm board or can multitask, i.e. solving a problem about labor for one business while driving to work at another. Why not utilize this time to benefit us? Before I bought my business and in my largest planning stages, I was ALWAYS thinking about ANYTHING to do with my plan. Literally, I would just sit there staring at my wall of lists and notes trying to think of anything that could get in my way. From loan requirements to employee rewards. Retrain your mind.

A few more noteworthy quotes for this introduction:

"Empty your mind, be formless, shapeless — like water. Now you put water in a cup, it becomes the cup; you put water into a bottle it becomes the bottle; you put it in a teapot it becomes the teapot. Now water can flow or it can crash. Be water, my friend." - Bruce Lee.

Keep an open mind and change tasks if one bogs you down. While this process may have you feeling overwhelmed at times, stay positive. If necessary, take a break and focus on other things, but always come back! Believe you can become whoever you want to be and be open to change and possibilities that may not seem "exact" when you first see them.

"The opposite of courage is conformity" – President John F. Kennedy; "JFK"

I'm from outside a small city; a city in which some generations do the least work possible or get "hurt" on purpose. Their children do not know any better. They may never know any better. Men (and women) overall have become lazier and no longer chase their dreams, or they fail to realize their dreams CAN be real with hard work and determination.

I met an individual recently on a trip to Phoenix who was busting their butt waiting tables. I was impressed with their hard work and determination – refusing to become irritated at more work or nuisances. "They put you to work here, huh," I said. "Yep, they try to get as much work as possible out of the least amount of people here," he said. With some sort of confused positivism, I stated, "Well, that's America!" I was so impressed with his response to me. "No, that's the American Dream!" he said with a pep to his step and overwhelming positivity.

On February 2, 2018, speakers on the TED Talk Hour on NPR discussed how slowing down can be beneficial in certain ways. I, like one of the speakers, always find my mind moving at 100 miles per hour. I like to solve problems as quickly, while effectively, as humanly possible. They spoke that some procrastination can be helpful in improving creativity. Starting a project or "Chapter" in this guide and then putting it aside to keep your brain working on it in the background (subconsciously) can HELP come up with creative ideas and thoughts. Do not however procrastinate too long or it will become debilitating and you may never finish it! Deliberately control your thoughts to become who you want to be.

"You have nothing to lose but you have everything to gain" – Earl Nightingale

---

If you listened to *The Strangest Secret*, you heard about Earl Nightingale's 30-day test. For this test, you are to write on a card what it is that you want and look at it regularly. Frequently solidifying the necessity for change and keeping it in the forefront of your mind. I challenge you to create a card with your vow and carry it daily to keep it at the forefront of your mind while you complete this guide. Make it two sided so the other side can list whichever chapter or project you are working on consciously and subconsciously.

Six Steps to Realize Success – Dr Harold Fink

Earl Nightingale also mentions Dr Harold Fink's Six Steps to Realize Success, and they are well worth putting in this guide as helpful motivation:

1. Set yourself a definite goal.
2. Quit running yourself down.
3. Stop thinking of all the reasons why you cannot be successful, and instead, think of all the reasons why you can.
4. Trace your attitude back through your childhood, and try to discover where you first got the idea you couldn't be successful, if that's the way you've been thinking.
5. Change the image you have of yourself by writing out a description of the person you would like to be.
6. Act the part of the successful person you have decided to become!

Why? Well, the smartest people I know solve their issues, create their plans and organize their thoughts on white boards. Think of it as a sort of mind map. Trying to plot turn by turn navigation from Buffalo, NY to Dallas, TX in your mind would be difficult. Taking a large printed map however and tracing the route with a highlighter would be working smarter not harder. Think of white boards in this fashion; your *Google Maps*.

To find my career choice it was important for me to keep my thoughts organized in different categories of a chart. There are so many different aspects to finding the right path! There are two blank charts at the end of this chapter for your "working thoughts" and "final draft." The copy on page 112 is for the future – think retirement, a second career, or another future life change.

If you write something in a column on your white board or working thoughts copy, you reword it a few times and it ends up staying in that column, put in on your final draft. Don't write anything prematurely onto this page. If you are like me, your first word will be far from the last one you choose to explain yourself. That one word can, and should, be broken into multiple thoughts.

This white board/chart serves as your minds "base camp." Rewording with dry erase markers makes things easy. While going through the categories in this guide, if you think of something that you want to include, but goes into another category, stick it in there. Even if it doesn't end up being the right category when you get there, it doesn't matter. **Don't lose the thought**. Write down the word or idea you have, and allow it to sit there and grow with conscious and subconscious thought around it. Don't be afraid to sit, stare at and contemplate your chart frequently.

DID YOU CREATE YOUR "VOW REMINDER CARD"?

ARE YOU DETERMINED TO MOVE FORWARD POSITIVELY?

Now, here is a breakdown of the categories required to find the career you deserve:

CHAPTER 1 –
      INTERESTS   - Majors or careers you are already considering.

CHAPTER 2 –
      OH HECK NO!   - Aspects you refuse to be part of your everyday life.

CHAPTER 3 –
      HOBBIES   - Personal activities for pleasure.

CHAPTER 4 –
      EXPERIENCE &   -Work history, knowledge, skills and abilities.
      BACKGROUND

CHAPTER 5 –
      ENVIRONMENT   - Who, What, When, Where, Why, How?

CHAPTER 6 –
      WANT   - What we would like to have but can live without.

CHAPTER 7 –
      REQUIREMENTS   - Things that unequivocally MUST be included.

CHAPTER 8 –
      ON THE SIDE   - Careers we may like to pursue on a part time basis.

CHAPTER 9 -
      CAREER   - Careers worth "testing."
      POSSIBILITIES

CHAPTER 10 -
      MOVING   - What do you do now?
      FORWARD

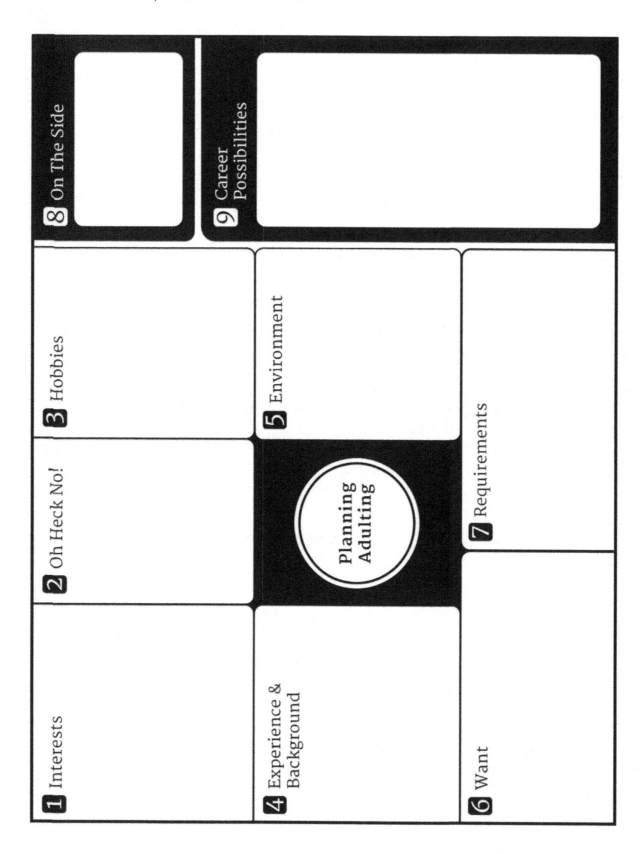

1 Interests

2 Oh Heck No!

3 Hobbies

4 Experience & Background

5 Environment

Planning Adulting

6 Want

7 Requirements

8 On The Side

9 Career Possibilities

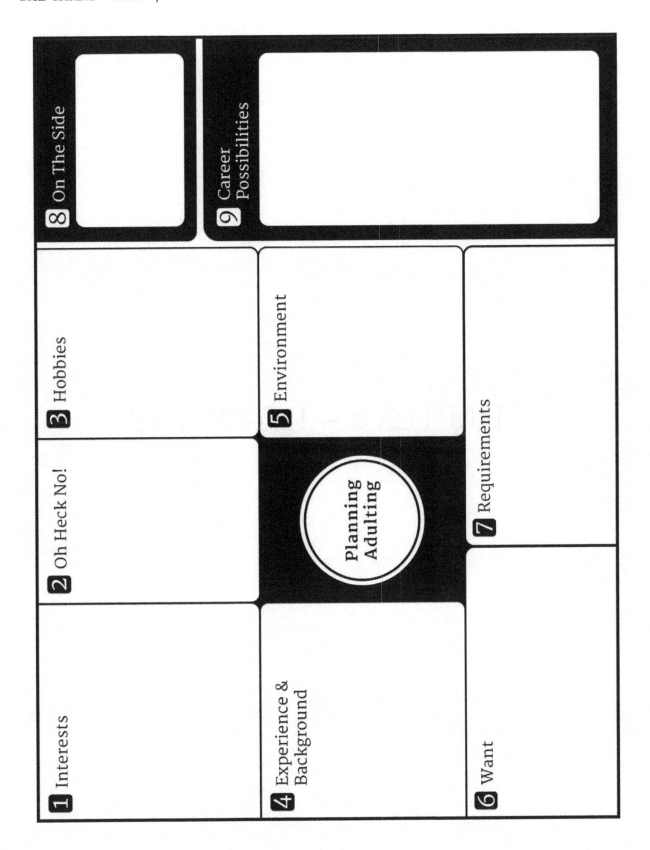

CHAPTER 1 – INTERESTS

Majors or careers you are already considering.

Ok...finally...here we go!!

Break it all down first, get it out of your system. Probably better than half of you filled out one of your charts before you read more than a few pages, or perhaps you didn't read anything first! However, going through this process is required to truly uncover the career you deserve. Remember - **when something important comes to your mind**, consult the Contents table for which category to put it in if necessary. **Write it down** while it is in the front of your mind.

My first category in the creation of this guide was for careers I already knew I might be interested in. I knew I was interested in being my own boss, so Entrepreneur was first on my list. My brother is a Helicopter pilot and that could provide an opportunity. I knew that I liked managing others, so I also put a general thought – management. I also added Police Officer because that's what I wanted to be in High School – don't forget your younger self's dream!

Before putting a whole lot of thought into what else you could do – you probably already have ideas. Is your mother a nurse and you've always thought about following in her shoes? Write it down. Don't think it's a real option? Write it down anyways. Maybe you'll find later that you always thought about following her steps because you liked her stories of helping people; maybe this will spark the idea of opening a marketing business to help busy small businesses spend their money wisely. Different than mom's career? Yes. Sparked by your thought of something you almost discounted? Yes! Write it down!

Everyone had a childhood dream or two! Even if it was a brief phase of our life. Doctor, astronaut, painter. It may be so far back in your memory you can't remember it, but what was it? Ask your parents, past teachers and friends. It may even seem too childish now to consider, but perhaps what it stood for isn't. I at one point wanted to chase tornado's! (O.K. you caught me, that was because of the movie *Twister* – but hey, I even memorized cloud patterns and category types).

 DID YOU ASK *PEOPLE* FROM YOUR LIFE WHAT YOUR DREAMS WERE?

YOUNGER ASPIRATIONS MATTER!

> "Life should be an exciting adventure, it should never be a bore. You should be glad to get up in the morning and get out of bed, ready for the day." - UNKNOWN

What gets your blood flowing (in a good way) when you do it? Mine was buying and selling cars, trucks, boats, RV's, anything with a motor. I only did it for myself, but my second business was doing this for others. I absolutely love it, but it's a very difficult business to be in and I knew it wasn't a full-time career for me.

What makes you the most excited to get out of bed? Can't sleep the night before your public speaking class because your excited to "rile everyone up"? Write it down!

What gets your blood flowing (in a good way) when you do it?

_____

_____

What makes you the most excited to get out of bed?

_____

_____

 DID YOU UPDATE YOUR CHART?

Think back to your **favorite job**. What felt most meaningful and satisfying? Do any specific events, days or situations stick out more positively? Now think back to your least favorite job. Why did you dislike it so much? Are there certain events that bothered you? Was is it a mentality? Was the job a means to an end? Why did you do it in the first place? If you think of something for another category but not sure it's the right category, throw it in there anyways! It can always be moved.

What felt most meaningful and satisfying?

_____

_____

Do any specific events, days, or situations stick out more positively?

_____

_____

Now think back to your **least favorite job**. Why did you dislike it?

_____

_____

Are there certain events that bothered you?

_____

_____

Was there a certain mentality? Was it a job that was a means to an end? Why did you do it?

_____

_____

Be vague! I found my number one career choice to be owning my own business; and I am glad I left that open to any type of business. I struggled for years on failed business ideas, but persevering paid off. Write down any idea you find, as general as you can, so it can grow into the career you deserve!

But be specific! Put yourself in the shoes of each career and consider it. Why would you like it? Why wouldn't you? Don't simply write off an idea because it doesn't sound perfect at first; that's like judging a book by its cover. One career that sparks a little negative thought in the back of your mind may be overcome by a gigantic list of positives once you imagine yourself doing it.

GO ONLINE TO WWW.CAREERPLANNER.COM.

DO THE TESTS! WHAT DID YOU FIND?

Check out this awesome career list mostly provided by CareerPlanner.com – a fantastic resource for Career Tests and Career Counseling (https://www.careerplanner.com/ListOfCareers.cfm):

TAKE YOUR TIME ON THIS LIST AND CONSIDER ANY OPTION,

DO NOT "GRAZE" OVER. THIS SHOULD TAKE HOURS!

PUT YOURSELF IN EACH CAREER'S SHOES & LOOK IT UP!

EVEN IF IT DOESN'T SOUND PERFECT, CIRCLE IT!

Accountants and Auditors
Actors
Actuaries
Acupuncturists
Administrative Law Judges, Adjudicators, and Hearing Officers
Administrative Services
Admin Services Managers
Adult Literacy, Remedial Education, and GED Teachers
Advertising and Promotions
Advertising Sales Agents
Aerospace Operations
Aerospace Engineers
Agents and Business Managers of Artists, Performers, and Athletes
Agricultural and Food Science Technicians
Agricultural Crop Farm Managers
Agricultural Engineers
Agricultural Equipment Operators
Agricultural Inspectors
Agricultural Sciences Teachers
Agricultural Technicians
Agricultural Workers
Air Crew Members
Air Crew Officers
Air Traffic Controllers
Aircraft Body and Structure Repairers
Aircraft Cargo Handling

Supervisors
Aircraft Engine Specialists
Aircraft Launch and Recovery Specialists
Aircraft Mechanics and Service Technicians
Aircraft Rigging Assemblers
Aircraft Systems Assemblers
Airfield Operations Specialists
Airframe-and-Power-Plant Mechanics
Airline Pilots, Copilots, and Flight Engineers
Allergists and Immunologists
Ambulance Drivers and Attendants
Amusement and Recreation Attendants
Anesthesiologist Assistants
Anesthesiologists
Animal Breeders
Animal Control Workers
Animal Scientists
Animal Trainers
Anthropologists
Archeologists
Anthropology and Archeology
Appraisers and Assessors of Real Estate
Aquacultural Managers
Arbitrators, Mediators, and Conciliators
Architects, Except Landscape and Naval
Architectural and Civil Drafters

Architecture Teachers
Archivists
Area, Ethnic, and Cultural Studies Teachers
Armored Assault Vehicle Members
Art Directors
Art Therapists
Art, Drama, and Music Teachers, Postsecondary
Assessors
Astronomers
Athletes and Sports Competitors
Athletic Trainers
Atmospheric and Space Scientists
Atmospheric, Earth, Marine, and Space Sciences Teachers
Audio and Video Equipment Technicians
Audiologists
Audio-Visual Collections Specialists
Auditors
Automatic Teller Machine Servicers
Automotive Body and Related Repairers
Automotive Engineers
Automotive Glass Installers and Repairers
Automotive Master Mechanics
Automotive Service Technicians
Automotive Specialty Technicians

Auxiliary Equipment Operators, Power
Aviation Inspectors
Avionics Technicians
Baggage Porters and Bellhops
Bailiffs
Bakers
Bakers, Bread and Pastry
Bakers, Manufacturing
Barbers
Baristas
Bartenders
Battery Repairers
Bench Workers, Jewelry
Bicycle Repairers
Bill and Account Collectors
Billing and Posting Clerks and Machine Operators
Billing, Cost, and Rate Clerks
Billing, Posting, and Calculating Machine Operators
Bindery Machine Operators and Tenders
Bindery Workers
Biochemists and Biophysicists
Biofuels Production Managers
Biofuels/Biodiesel Tech & Product Development
Bioinformatics Scientists, Technicians
Biological Science Teachers
Biological Technicians
Biologists
Biomass Plant Technicians
Biomass Power Plant Managers
Biomedical Engineers
Biophysicists
Biostatisticians Boat Builders and Shipwrights
Boiler Operators and Tenders, Low Pressure
Boilermakers
Bookbinders
Bookkeeping, Accounting, and Auditing Clerks
Brattice Builders
Brazers
Brickmasons and Blockmasons
Bridge and Lock Tenders
Broadcast News Analysts
Broadcast Technicians
Brokerage Clerks
Budget Analysts
Buffing and Polishing Set-Up Operators
Building Cleaning Workers
Bus and Truck Mechanics and Diesel Engine Specialists

Bus Drivers, School
Bus Drivers, Transit and Intercity
Business Continuity Planners
Business Intelligence Analysts
Business Operations Specialists
Business Teachers
Butchers and Meat Cutters
Cabinetmakers and Bench Carpenters
Calibration and Instrumentation Technicians
Camera and Photographic Equipment Repairers
Camera Operators
Camera Operators, Television, Video, and Motion Picture
Captains, Mates, and Pilots of Water Vessels
Caption Writers
Cardiovascular Technologists and Technicians
Cargo and Freight Agents
Carpenter Assemblers and Repairers
Carpenters
Carpet Installers
Cartographers and Photogrammetrists
Cartoonists
Cashiers
Casting Machine Set-Up Operators
Ceiling Tile Installers
Cement Masons and Concrete Finishers
Cementing and Gluing Machine Operators and Tenders
Central Office and PBX Installers and Repairers
Central Office Operators
Chefs and Head Cooks
Chemical Engineers
Chemical Equipment Controllers and Operators
Chemical Equipment Operators and Tenders
Chemical Equipment Tenders
Chemical Plant and System Operators
Chemical Technicians
Chemistry Teachers
Chemists
Chief Executives
Chief Sustainability Officers
Child Care Workers
Child Support, Missing Persons, and Unemployment Insurance

Fraud Investigators
Child, Family, and School Social Workers
Chiropractors
Choreographers
City Planning Aides
Civil Drafters
Civil Engineering Technicians
Civil Engineers
Claims Adjusters, Examiners, and Investigators
Claims Examiners, Property and Casualty Insurance
Claims Takers, Unemployment Benefits
Cleaners of Vehicles and Equipment
Cleaning, Washing, and Metal Pickling Equipment Operators and Tenders
Clergy
Climate Change Analysts
Clinical Data Managers
Clinical Nurse Specialists
Clinical Psychologists
Clinical Research Coordinators
Clinical, Counseling, and School Psychologists
Coaches and Scouts
Coating, Painting, and Spraying Machine Operators and Tenders
Coating, Painting, and Spraying Machine Setters and Set-Up Operators
Coating, Painting, and Spraying Machine Setters, Operators, And Tenders
Coil Winders, Tapers, and Finishers
Coin, Vending, and Amusement Machine Servicers and Repairers
Combination Machine Tool Operators and Tenders, Metal and Plastic
Combination Machine Tool Setters and Set-Up Operators
Combined Food Preparation and Serving Workers, Including Fast Food
Command and Control Center Officers, Specialists
Commercial and Industrial Designers
Commercial Divers
Commercial Pilots
Communication Equipment

Mechanics, Installers, Repairers, Operators
Communications Teachers
Community and Social Service Specialists
Community Health Workers
Compensation and Benefits Managers
Compensation, Benefits, and Job Analysis Specialist
Compliance Managers
Compliance Officers, Except Agriculture, Construction, Health and Safety, and Transportation
Composers
Computer and Information Research Scientists
Computer and Information Scientists, Research
Computer and Information Systems Managers
Computer Hardware Engineers
Computer Network Architects
Computer Network Support
Computer Operators
Computer Programmer
Computer Science Teachers
Computer Security Specialists
Computer Software Engineers, Applications
Computer Software Engineers, Systems Software
Computer Specialists, All Other
Computer Support Specialists
Computer Systems Analyst
Computer Systems Engineers/Architects
Computer User Support Specialists
Computer, Automated Teller, and Office Machine Repairers
Computer-Controlled Machine Tool Operators, Metal and Plastic
Concierges
Conservation Scientists
Construction and Building Inspectors
Construction Carpenters
Construction Drillers
Construction Laborers
Construction Managers
Continuous Mining Machine Operators
Control and Valve Installers and Repairers
Conveyor Operators and Tenders
Cooks
Cooks, Institution and Cafeteria
Cooks, Private Household
Cooks, Restaurant
Cooks, Short Order
Cooling and Freezing Equipment Operators and Tenders
Copy Writers
Coroners
Correctional Officers and Jailers
Correspondence Clerks
Cost Estimators
Costume Attendants
Counseling Psychologists
Counselors
Counter and Rental Clerks
Counter Attendants, Cafeteria, Food Concession, and Coffee Shop
Couriers and Messengers
Court Clerks
Court Reporters
Court, Municipal, and License Clerks
Craft Artists
Crane and Tower Operators
Creative Writers
Credit Analysts
Credit Authorizers, Checkers, and Clerks
Credit Checkers
Criminal Investigators and Special Agents
Criminal Justice and Law Enforcement Teachers
Critical Care Nurses
Crossing Guards
Crushing, Grinding, and Polishing Machine Setters, Operators, and Tenders
Curators
Custom Tailors
Customer Service Representatives
Customs Brokers
Cutters and Trimmers, Hand
Cutting and Slicing Machine Operators and Tenders
Cutting and Slicing Machine Setters, Operators, and Tenders
Cutting, Punching, and Press Machine Setters, Operators, and Tenders, Metal and Plastic
Cytogenetic Technologists
Cytotechnologists
Dancers
Data Entry Keyers
Data Processing Equipment Repairers
Data Warehousing Specialists
Database Administrator
Database Administrators
Database Architects
Demonstrators and Product Promoters
Dental Assistants
Dental Hygienists
Dental Laboratory Technicians
Dentists
Dermatologists
Derrick Operators, Oil and Gas
Design Printing Machine Setters and Set-Up Operators
Designers
Desktop Publishers
Detectives and Criminal Investigators
Diagnostic Medical Sonographers
Dietetic Technicians
Dietitians and Nutritionists
Dining Room and Cafeteria Attendants and Bartender Helpers
Directors- Stage, Motion Pictures, Television, and Radio
Directors, Religious Activities and Education
Directory Assistance Operators
Dishwashers
Dispatchers, Except Police, Fire, and Ambulance
Distance Learning Coordinators
Document Management
Door-To-Door Sales Workers, News and Street Vendors, and Related Workers
Dot Etchers
Drafters
Dragline Operators
Dredge Operators
Drilling and Boring Machine Tool Setters, Operators, and Tenders, Metal and Plastic
Driver-Sales Workers
Drywall and Ceiling Tile Installers
Drywall Installers
Duplicating Machine Operators
Earth Drillers, Except Oil and Gas
Economics Teachers
Economists
Editors

Education Administrators
Education Teachers
Education, Training, and Library Workers
Educational Psychologists
Educational, Vocational, and School Counselors
Electric Home Appliance and Power Tool Repairers
Electric Meter Installers and Repairers
Electric Motor and Switch Assemblers and Repairers
Electric Motor, Power Tool, and Related Repairers
Electrical and Electronic Engineering Technicians
Electrical and Electronic Equipment Assemblers
Electrical and Electronic Inspectors and Testers
Electrical and Electronics Drafters
Electrical and Electronics Installers and Repairers, Transportation Equipment
Electrical and Electronics Repairers, Commercial and Industrial Equipment
Electrical and Electronics Repairers, Powerhouse, Substation, and Relay
Electrical Drafters
Electrical Engineering Technicians
Electrical Engineering Technologists
Electrical Engineers
Electrical Parts Reconditioners
Electrical Power-Line Installers and Repairers
Electricians
Electrolytic Plating and Coating Machine Operators and Tenders, Metal and Plastic
Electrolytic Plating and Coating Machine Setters and Set-Up Operators, Metal and Plastic
Electromechanical Engineering Technologists
Electromechanical Equipment Assemblers
Electro-Mechanical Technicians
Electronic Drafters
Electronic Equipment Installers and Repairers, Motor Vehicles
Electronic Home Entertainment Equipment Installers and

Repairers
Electronic Masking System Operators
Electronics Engineering Technicians
Electronics Engineering Technologists
Electronics Engineers, Except Computer
Electrotypers and Stereotypers
Elementary School Teachers, Except Special Education
Elevator Installers and Repairers
Eligibility Interviewers, Government Programs
Embalmers
Embossing Machine Operators
Emergency Management Specialists
Emergency Medical Technicians and Paramedics
Employment Interviewers, Private or Public Employment Service
Employment, Recruitment, and Placement Specialists
Endoscopy Technicians
Energy Auditors
Energy Brokers
Energy Engineers
Engine and Other Machine Assemblers
Engineering Managers
Engineering Teachers
Engineering Technicians, Except Drafters
Engineers
English Language and Literature Teachers
Engravers, Hand
Engravers--Carvers
Entertainers and Performers, Sports and Related Workers
Entertainment Attendants and Related Workers
Environmental Compliance Inspectors
Environmental Economists
Environmental Engineering Technicians
Environmental Engineers
Environmental Restoration Planners
Environmental Science and Protection Technicians, Including Health
Environmental Science Teachers
Environmental Scientists and

Specialists, Including Health
Epidemiologists
Equal Opportunity Representatives and Officers
Etchers and Engravers
Excavating and Loading Machine and Dragline Operators
Executive Secretaries and Administrative Assistants
Exercise Physiologists
Exhibit Designers
Explosives Workers, Ordnance Handling Experts, and Blasters
Extraction Workers
Extruding and Drawing Machine Setters, Operators, and Tenders, Metal and Plastic
Extruding and Forming Machine Operators and Tenders, Synthetic or Glass Fibers
Extruding, Forming, Pressing, and Compacting Machine Operators and Tenders
Fabric and Apparel Patternmakers
Fabric Menders
Fallers
Family and General Practitioners
Farm and Home Management Advisors
Farm and Ranch Managers
Farm Equipment Mechanics
Farm Labor Contractor
Farm, Ranch, and Other Agricultural Managers
Farmers and Ranchers
Farmworkers and Laborers, Crop, Nursery, and Greenhouse
Farmworkers, Farm and Ranch Animals
Fashion Designers
Fence Erectors
Fiber Product Cutting Machine Setters and Set-Up Operators
Fiberglass Laminators and Fabricators
File Clerks
Film and Video Editors
Film Laboratory Technicians
Financial Analysts
Financial Examiners
Financial Managers
Financial Managers, Branch or Department
Financial Quantitative Analysts
Financial Specialists

Fine Artists, Including Painters, Sculptors, and Illustrators
Fire Fighters
Fire Inspectors and Investigators
Fire Investigators
Fire-Prevention and Protection Engineers
First-Line Supervisors – Agricultural Crop Workers
First-Line Supervisors - Animal Care Workers, Except Livestock
First-Line Supervisors - Animal Husbandry Workers
First-Line Supervisors - Fishery Workers
First-Line Supervisors – Horticultural Workers
First-Line Supervisors – Landscaping Workers
First-Line Supervisors - Logging Workers
First-Line Supervisors – Construction Trades Workers
First-Line Supervisors – Extractive Workers
First-Line Supervisors of Agricultural Crop and Horticultural Workers
First-Line Supervisors of Animal Husbandry and Animal Care Workers
First-Line Supervisors, Administrative Support
First-Line Supervisors, Customer Service
First-Line Supervisors- Air Crew Members
First-Line Supervisors- Managers of All Other Tactical Operations Specialists
First-Line Supervisors- Managers of Construction Trades and Extraction Workers
First-Line Supervisors- of Correctional Officers
First-Line Supervisors- Farming, Fishing, and Forestry Workers
First-Line Supervisors- Fire Fighting and Prevention Workers
First-Line Supervisors- Food Preparation and Serving Workers
First-Line Supervisors- Helpers, Laborers, and Material Movers, Hand
First-Line Supervisors-

Housekeeping and Janitorial Workers
First-Line Supervisors- Landscaping, Lawn Service, and Groundskeeping Workers
First-Line Supervisors- Mechanics, Installers, and Repairers
First-Line Supervisors- Non-Retail Sales Workers
First-Line Supervisors- Office and Administrative Support Workers
First-Line Supervisors- Personal Service Workers
First-Line Supervisors- Police and Detectives
First-Line Supervisors- Production and Operating Workers
First-Line Supervisors- Retail Sales Workers
First-Line Supervisors- Transportation and Material-Moving Machine and Vehicle Operators
First-Line Supervisors- Weapons Specialists--Crew Members
First-Line Supervisors- Protective Service Workers
Fish and Game Wardens
Fish Hatchery Managers
Fishers and Related Fishing Workers
Fitness and Wellness Coordinators
Fitness Trainers and Aerobics Instructors
Fitters, Structural Metal-Precision
Flight Attendants
Floor Layers, Except Carpet, Wood, and Hard Tiles
Floor Sanders and Finishers
Floral Designers
Food and Tobacco Roasting, Baking, and Drying Machine Operators and Tenders
Food Batchmakers
Food Cooking Machine Operators and Tenders
Food Preparation and Serving Related Workers
Food Scientists and Technologists
Food Servers, Nonrestaurant
Food Service Managers

Foreign Language and Literature Teachers
Forensic Science Technicians
Forest and Conservation Technicians
Forest and Conservation Workers
Forest Fire Fighters
Forest Fire Fighting and Prevention Supervisors
Forest Fire Inspectors and Prevention Specialists
Foresters
Forestry and Conservation Science Teachers
Forging Machine Setters, Operators, and Tenders, Metal and Plastic
Foundry Mold and Coremakers
Frame Wirers, Central Office
Fraud Examiners, Investigators and Analysts
Freight and Cargo Inspectors
Freight Forwarders
Freight Inspectors
Freight, Stock, and Material Movers, Hand
Fuel Cell Engineers
Fuel Cell Technicians
Fundraisers
Funeral Attendants
Funeral Directors
Furnace, Kiln, Oven, Drier, and Kettle Operators and Tenders
Furniture Finishers
Gaming and Sports Book Writers and Runners
Gaming Cage Workers
Gaming Change Persons and Booth Cashiers
Gaming Dealers
Gaming Managers
Gaming Service Workers
Gaming Supervisors
Gaming Surveillance Officers and Gaming Investigators
Gas Appliance Repairers
Gas Compressor and Gas Pumping Station Operators
Gas Compressor Operators
Gas Plant Operators
Gas Pumping Station Operators
Gaugers
Gem and Diamond Workers
General and Operations Managers
General Farmworkers
Genetic Counselors

Geneticists
Geodetic Surveyors
Geographers
Geographic Information Systems Technicians
Geography Teachers
Geological and Petroleum Technicians
Geological Data Technicians
Geological Sample Test Technicians
Geologists
Geoscientists, Except Hydrologists and Geographers
Geospatial Information Scientists and Technologists
Geothermal Production Managers
Geothermal Technicians
Glass Blowers, Molders, Benders, and Finishers
Glass Cutting Machine Setters and Set-Up Operators
Glaziers
Government Property Inspectors and Investigators
Government Service Executives
Grader, Bulldozer, and Scraper Operators
Graders and Sorters, Agricultural Products
Graduate Teaching Assistants
Graphic Designers
Green Marketers
Grinding, Lapping, Polishing, and Buffing Machine Tool Setters, Operators, and Tenders
Grips and Set-Up Workers, Motion Picture Sets, Studios, and Stages
Grounds Maintenance Workers
Hairdressers, Hairstylists, and Cosmetologists
Hand and Portable Power Tool Repairers
Hand Compositors and Typesetters
Hazardous Materials Removal Workers
Health and Safety Engineers, Except Mining Safety Engineers and Inspectors
Health Diagnosing and Treating Practitioners
Health Educators
Health Specialties Teachers
Health Technologists and Technicians

Healthcare Practitioners and Technical Workers
Healthcare Support Workers
Hearing Aid Specialists
Heat Treating Equipment Setters, Operators, and Tenders
Heat Treating, Annealing, and Tempering Machine Operators and Tenders
Heating, Air Conditioning, and Refrigeration Mechanics and Installers
Helpers, Construction Trades
Helpers-Brickmasons, Blockmasons, Stonemasons, and Tile and Marble Setters
Helpers-Carpenters
Helpers-Electricians
Helpers-Extraction Workers
Helpers-Installation, Maintenance, and Repair Workers
Helpers-Painters, Paperhangers, Plasterers, and Stucco Masons
Helpers-Pipelayers, Plumbers, Pipefitters, and Steamfitters
Helpers-Production Workers
Helpers-Roofers
Highway Maintenance Workers
Highway Patrol Pilots
Historians
History Teachers
Histotechnologists and Histologic Technicians
Hoist and Winch Operators
Home Appliance Installers
Home Appliance Repairers
Home Economics Teachers
Home Health Aides
Hospitalists
Hosts and Hostesses, Restaurant, Lounge, and Coffee Shop
Hotel, Motel, and Resort Desk Clerks
Housekeeping Supervisors
Human Factors Engineers and Ergonomists
Human Resources Assistants, Except Payroll and Timekeeping
Human Resources Manager
Human Resources, Training, and Labor Relations Specialists
Hunters and Trappers
Hydroelectric Plant Technicians
Hydroelectric Production Managers

Hydrologists
Immigration and Customs Inspectors
Industrial Ecologists
Industrial Engineers
Industrial Machinery Mechanics
Industrial Production Managers
Industrial Safety and Health Engineers
Industrial Truck and Tractor Operators
Industrial-Organizational Psychologists
Infantry
Infantry Officers
Informatics Nurse Specialists
Information and Record Clerks
Information Security Analysts
Information Technology Project Managers
Inspectors, Testers, Sorters, Samplers, and Weighers
Installation, Maintenance, and Repair Workers
Instructional Coordinators
Instructional Designers and Technologists
Insulation Workers, Floor, Ceiling, and Wall
Insulation Workers, Mechanical
Insurance Adjusters, Examiners, and Investigators
Insurance Appraisers, Auto Damage
Insurance Claims and Policy Processing Clerks
Insurance Claims Clerks
Insurance Policy Processing Clerks
Insurance Sales Agents
Insurance Underwriters
Intelligence Analysts
Interior Designers
Internists, General
Interpreters and Translators
Interviewers, Except Eligibility and Loan
Investment Fund Managers
Investment Underwriters
Irradiated-Fuel Handlers
Janitorial Supervisors
Janitors and Cleaners
Jewelers
Jewelers and Precious Stone and Metal Workers
Job Printers
Judges, Magistrate Judges, and Magistrates

Judicial Law Clerks
Keyboard Instrument Repairers
and Tuners Kindergarten
Teachers
Labor Relations Specialists
Laborers and Freight, Stock, and
Material Movers, Hand
Landscape Architects
Landscaping and
Groundskeeping Workers
Lathe and Turning Machine
Tool Setters, Operators, and
Tenders
Laundry and Drycleaning
Machine Operators and
Tenders
Laundry and Dry-Cleaning
Workers
Law Clerks
Law Teachers
Lawn Service Managers
Lawyers
Lay-Out Workers
Legal Secretaries
Legal Support Workers
Legislators
Letterpress Setters and Set-Up
Operators
Librarians
Library Assistants, Clerical
Library Science Teachers
Library Technicians
License Clerks
Licensed Practical and Licensed
Vocational Nurses
Licensing Examiners and
Inspectors
Life Scientists
Life, Physical, and Social
Science Technicians
Lifeguards, Ski Patrol, and
Other Recreational Protective
Service Workers
Loading Machine Operators,
Underground Mining
Loan Counselors
Loan Interviewers and Clerks
Loan Officers
Locker Room, Coatroom, and
Dressing Room Attendants
Locksmiths and Safe Repairers
Locomotive Engineers
Locomotive Firers
Lodging Managers
Log Graders and Scalers
Logging Equipment Operators
Logging Tractor Operators
Logging Workers

Logisticians
Logistics Analysts
Logistics Engineers
Logistics Managers
Loss Prevention Managers
Low Vision Therapists,
Orientation and Mobility
Specialists, and Vision
Rehabilitation Therapists
Machine Feeders and Offbearers
Machinists
Magnetic Resonance Imaging
Technologists
Maids and Housekeeping
Cleaners
Mail Clerks Mail Machine
Operators and Postal Service
Mail Machine Operators,
Preparation and Handling
Maintenance and Repair Worker
Maintenance Workers, Machinery
Makeup Artists, Theatrical and
Performance
Management Analysts
Managers, All Other
Manicurists and Pedicurists
Manufactured Building and
Mobile Home Installers
Manufacturing Engineering
Technologists
Manufacturing Engineers
Manufacturing Production
Technicians
Mapping Technicians
Marine Architects
Marine Cargo Inspectors
Marine Engineers
Marine Engineers and Naval
Architects
Market Research Analysts and
Marketing Specialists
Marketing Managers
Marking and Identification
Printing Machine Setters and
Set-Up Operators
Marking Clerks
Marriage and Family Therapists
Massage Therapists
Material Moving Workers
Materials Engineers
Materials Inspectors
Materials Scientists
Mates- Ship, Boat, and Barge
Mathematical Science
Occupations
Mathematical Science Teachers
Mathematical Technicians
Mathematicians

Meat, Poultry, and Fish Cutters
and Trimmers
Mechanical Door Repairers
Mechanical Drafters
Mechanical Engineering
Technicians
Mechanical Engineering
Technologists
Mechanical Engineers
Mechanical Inspectors
Mechatronics Engineers
Media and Communication
Equipment Workers
Medical and Clinical Laboratory
Technicians
Medical and Clinical Laboratory
Technologists
Medical and Health Services
Managers
Medical and Public Health
Social Workers
Medical Appliance Technicians
Medical Assistants
Medical Equipment Preparers
Medical Equipment Repairers
Medical Records and Health
Information Technicians
Medical Scientists, Except
Epidemiologists
Medical Secretaries
Medical Transcriptionists
Meeting and Convention
Planners
Mental Health and Substance
Abuse Social Workers
Mental Health Counselors
Merchandise Displayers and
Window Trimmers
Metal Fabricators, Structural
Metal Products
Metal Molding, Coremaking,
and Casting Machine Operators
and Tenders
Metal Molding, Coremaking,
and Casting Machine Setters
and Set-Up Operators
Metal Workers and Plastic
Workers
Metal-Refining Furnace
Operators and Tenders
Meter Mechanics
Meter Readers, Utilities
Methane Landfill Gas
Generation System
Technicians
Methane/Landfill Gas
Collection System Operators
Microbiologists

Microsystems Engineers
Middle School Teachers
Midwives
Military Enlisted Tactical
Operations and Air--Weapons
Specialists and Crew Members
Military Officer Special and
Tactical Operations Leaders—
Managers
Milling and Planing Machine
Setters, Operators, and Tenders
Millwrights
Mine Cutting and Channeling
Machine Operators
Mining and Geological
Engineers, Including Mining
Safety Engineers
Mining Machine Operators
Mixing and Blending Machine
Setters, Operators, and Tenders
Mobile Heavy Equipment
Mechanics, Except Engines
Model and Mold Makers,
Jewelry
Model Makers, Metal and
Plastic
Model Makers, Wood
Models
Mold Makers, Hand
Molders, Shapers, and Casters,
Except Metal and Plastic
Molding and Casting Workers
Molding, Coremaking, and
Casting Machine Setters,
Operators, and Tenders, Metal
and Plastic
Molecular and Cellular
Biologists
Morticians, Undertakers, and
Funeral Directors
Motion Picture Projectionists
Motor Vehicle Inspectors
Motor Vehicle Operators
Motorboat Mechanics
Motorboat Operators
Motorcycle Mechanics
Multi-Media Artists and
Animators
Multiple Machine Tool Setters,
Operators, and Tenders
Municipal Clerks
Municipal Fire Fighters
Municipal Fire Fighting and
Prevention Supervisors
Museum Technicians and
Conservators
Music Arrangers and
Orchestrators

Music Composers and Arrangers
Music Directors
Music Directors and Composers
Music Therapists
Musical Instrument Repairers
and Tuners
Musicians and Singers
Musicians, Instrumental
Nannies
Nanosystems Engineers
Nanotechnology Engineering
Technicians
Nanotechnology Engineering
Technologists
Natural Sciences Managers
Naturopathic Physicians
Network and Computer Systems
Administrators
Network Systems and Data
Communications Analysts
Neurodiagnostic Technologists
Neurologists
Neuropsychologists
New Accounts Clerks
Non-Destructive Testing
Specialists
Nonelectrolytic Plating and
Coating Machine Operators
and Tenders
Nonfarm Animal Caretakers
Nuclear Engineers
Nuclear Equipment Operations
Nuclear Medicine Physicians
Nuclear Medicine Technologists
Nuclear Monitoring Technicians
Nuclear Power Reactor
Operators
Nuclear Technicians
Numerical Control Machine
Tool Operators and Tenders
Numerical Tool and Process
Control Programmers
Nurse Anesthetists
Nurse Midwives
Nurse Practitioners
Nursery and Greenhouse
Manager
Nursery and Greenhouse
Managers
Nursery Workers
Nursing Aides, Orderlies, and
Attendants
Nursing Assistants
Nursing Instructors and
Teachers
Obstetricians and Gynecologists
Occupational Health and Safety
Specialists

Occupational Health and Safety
Technicians
Occupational Therapist Aides
Occupational Therapist
Assistants
Occupational Therapists
Office and Administrative
Support Workers
Office Clerks
Office Machine and Cash
Register Servicers
Office Machine Operators,
Except Computer
Offset Lithographic Press
Setters and Set-Up Operators
Online Merchants
Operating Engineers
Operating Engineers and Other
Construction Equipment
Operators
Operations Research Analysts
Ophthalmic Laboratory
Technicians
Ophthalmic Medical
Technicians
Ophthalmic Medical
Technologists
Ophthalmologists
Optical Instrument Assemblers
Opticians, Dispensing
Optometrists
Oral and Maxillofacial Surgeons
Order Clerks
Order Fillers, Wholesale and
Retail Sales
Orderlies
Ordinary Seamen and Marine
Oilers
Orthodontists
Orthoptists
Orthotists and Prosthetists
Outdoor Power Equipment and
Other Small Engine Mechanics
Packaging and Filling Machine
Operators and Tenders
Packers and Packagers, Hand
Painters and Illustrators
Painters, Construction and
Maintenance
Painters, Transportation
Equipment
Painting, Coating, and
Decorating Workers
Pantograph Engravers
Paper Goods Machine Setters,
Operators, and Tenders
Paperhangers
Paralegals and Legal Assistants

Park Naturalists
Parking Enforcement Workers
Parking Lot Attendants
Parts Salespersons
Paste-Up Workers
Pathologists
Patient Representatives
Patternmakers
Patternmakers, Wood
Paving, Surfacing, and Tamping Equipment Operators
Payroll and Timekeeping Clerks
Pediatricians
Percussion Instrument Repairers and Tuners
Personal and Home Care Aides
Personal Care and Service Worker
Personal Financial Advisors
Personnel Recruiters
Pest Control Workers
Pesticide Handlers, Sprayers, and Applicators, Vegetation
Petroleum Engineers
Petroleum Pump System Operators, Refinery Operators, and Gaugers
Petroleum Refinery and Control Panel Operators
Pewter Casters and Finishers
Pharmacists
Pharmacy Aides
Pharmacy Technicians
Philosophy and Religion Teachers
Phlebotomists
Photoengravers
Photoengraving and Lithographing Machine Operators and Tenders
Photographers
Photographers, Scientific
Photographic Hand Developers
Photographic Process Workers and Processing Machine Operators
Photographic Reproduction Technicians
Photographic Retouchers and Restorers
Photonics Engineers
Photonics Technicians
Physical Medicine and Rehabilitation Physicians
Physical Scientists
Physical Therapist Aides
Physical Therapist Assistants
Physical Therapists

Physician Assistants
Physicians and Surgeons
Physicists
Physics Teachers
Pile-Driver Operators
Pilots, Ship
Pipe Fitters
Pipelayers
Plant and System Operators
Plant Scientists
Plasterers and Stucco Masons
Plastic Molding and Casting Machine Operators and Tenders
Plastic Molding and Casting Machine Setters and Set-Up Operators
Plate Finishers
Platemakers
Plating and Coating Machine Setters, Operators, and Tenders
Plumbers
Plumbers, Pipefitters, and Steamfitters
Podiatrists
Poets and Lyricists
Poets, Lyricists and Creative Writers
Police and Sheriffs Patrol Officers
Police Detectives
Police Identification and Records Officers
Police Patrol Officers
Police, Fire, and Ambulance Dispatchers
Political Science Teachers
Political Scientists
Postal Service Clerks
Postal Service Mail Carriers
Postal Service Mail Sorters, Processors, and Processing Machine Operators
Postmasters and Mail Superintendents
Postsecondary Teachers
Potters
Pourers and Casters, Metal
Power Distributors and Dispatchers
Power Generating Plant Operators, Except Auxiliary Equipment Operators
Power Plant Operators
Precious Metal Workers
Precision Agriculture Technicians
Precision Devices Inspectors

and Testers
Precision Dyers
Precision Etchers and Engravers, Hand or Machine
Precision Instrument and Equipment Repairers
Precision Lens Grinders and Polishers
Precision Mold and Pattern Casters, except Nonferrous Metals
Precision Pattern and Die Casters, Nonferrous Metals
Precision Printing Workers
Prepress Technician
Prepress Technicians and Workers
Preschool Teachers
Press and Press Brake Machine Setters and Set-Up Operators, Metal and Plastic
Pressers, Hand
Pressing Machine Operators
Pressure Vessel Inspectors
Preventive Medicine Physicians
Print Binding and Finishing Workers
Printing Machine Operators
Printing Press Machine Operators and Tenders
Printing Press Operators
Private Detectives and Investigators
Private Sector Executives
Probation Officers and Correctional Treatment Specialists
Procurement Clerks
Producers and Directors
Product Safety Engineers
Production Helpers
Production Inspectors, Testers, Graders, Sorters, Samplers, Weighers
Production Laborers
Production Workers, All Other
Production, Planning, and Expediting Clerks
Professional Photographers
Program Directors
Proofreaders and Copy Markers
Property, Real Estate, and Community Association Managers
Prosthodontists
Protective Service Workers
Psychiatric Aides
Psychiatric Technicians

Psychiatrists
Psychologists
Psychology Teachers, Postsecondary
Public Address System and Other Announcers
Public Relations Managers
Public Relations Specialists
Public Transportation Inspectors
Pump Operators
Punching Machine Setters and Set-Up Operators
Purchasing Agents and Buyers, Farm Products
Purchasing Agents, Except Wholesale, Retail, and Farm Products
Purchasing Managers
Quality Control Analysts
Quality Control Systems Managers
Radar and Sonar Technicians
Radiation Therapists
Radio and Television Announcers
Radio Frequency Identification Device Specialists
Radio Mechanics
Radio Operators
Radiologic Technicians
Radiologic Technologists
Radiologists
Rail Car Repairers
Rail Transportation Workers
Rail Yard Engineers, Dinkey Operators, and Hostlers
Railroad Brake, Signal, and Switch Operators
Railroad Conductors and Yardmasters
Railroad Inspectors
Railroad Yard Workers
Rail-Track Laying and Maintenance Equipment Operators
Range Managers
Real Estate Brokers
Real Estate Sales Agents
Receptionists and Information Clerks
Recreation and Fitness Studies Teachers
Recreation Workers
Recreational Therapists
Recreational Vehicle Service Technicians
Recycling and Reclamation Workers

Recycling Coordinators
Reed or Wind Instrument Repairers and Tuners
Refractory Materials Repairers, Except Brickmasons
Refrigeration Mechanics
Refuse and Recyclable Material Collectors
Registered Nurses
Regulatory Affairs Managers
Regulatory Affairs Specialists
Rehabilitation Counselors
Reinforcing Iron and Rebar Workers
Religious Workers
Remote Sensing Scientists and Technologists
Remote Sensing Technicians
Reporters and Correspondents
Reservation and Transportation Ticket Agents
Reservation and Transportation Ticket Agents and Travel Clerks
Residential Advisors
Respiratory Therapists
Respiratory Therapy Technicians
Retail Loss Prevention Specialists
Retail Salespersons
Riggers
Risk Management Specialists
Robotics Engineers
Robotics Technicians
Rock Splitters, Quarry
Rolling Machine Setters, Operators, and Tenders, Metal and Plastic
Roof Bolters, Mining
Roofers
Rotary Drill Operators, Oil and Gas
Rough Carpenters
Roustabouts, Oil and Gas
Sailors and Marine Oilers
Sales Agents, Financial Services
Sales Agents, Securities and Commodities
Sales and Related Workers
Sales Engineers
Sales Managers
Sales-Agricultural
Sales-Chemical and Pharmaceutical
Sales-Electrical/Electronic
Sales-Instruments
Sales-Mechanical Equipment

and Supplies
Sales-Medical
Sales-Services, All Other
Sales-Wholesale and Manufacturing, Except Technical and Scientific Products
Sales-Wholesale and Manufacturing, Technical and Scientific Products
Sawing Machine Operators and Tenders
Sawing Machine Setters and Set-Up Operators
Scanner Operators
Screen Printing Machine Setters and Set-Up Operators
Sculptors
Search Marketing Strategists
Secondary School Teachers
Secretaries, Except Legal, Medical, and Executive
Securities and Commodities Traders
Securities, Commodities, and Financial Services Sales Agents
Security and Fire Alarm Systems Installers
Security Guards
Security Management Specialists
Security Managers
Segmental Pavers
Self-Enrichment Education Teachers
Semiconductor Processors
Separating, Filtering, Clarifying, Precipitating, and Still Machine Setters, Operators, and Tenders
Septic Tank Servicers and Sewer Pipe Cleaners
Service Station Attendants
Service Unit Operators, Oil, Gas, and Mining
Set and Exhibit Designers
Set Designers
Sewers, Hand
Sewing Machine Operators
Sheet Metal Workers
Sheriffs and Deputy Sheriffs
Ship and Boat Captains
Ship Carpenters and Joiners
Ship Engineers
Shipping, Receiving, and Traffic Clerks
Shoe and Leather Workers and Repairers

Shoe Machine Operators and Tenders
Shop and Alteration Tailors
Shuttle Car Operators
Signal and Track Switch Repairers
Silversmiths
Singers
Sketch Artists
Skin Care Specialists
Slaughterers and Meat Packers
Slot Key Persons
Social and Community Service Managers
Social and Human Service Assistants
Social Science Research Assistants
Social Sciences Teachers
Social Scientists and Related Workers
Social Work Teachers
Social Workers
Sociologists
Sociology Teachers
Software Developers, Applications
Software Developers, Systems Software
Software Quality Assurance Engineers and Testers
Soil and Plant Scientists
Soil Conservationists
Soil Scientists
Solar Energy Installation Managers
Solar Energy Systems Engineers
Solar Photovoltaic Installers
Solar Sales Representatives and Assessors
Solar Thermal Installers and Technicians
Solderers and Brazers
Soldering and Brazing Machine Operators and Tenders
Sound Engineering Technicians
Spa Managers
Special Education Teacher
Special Education Teachers, Kindergarten and Elementary School
Special Education Teachers
Special Forces
Special Forces Officers
Speech-Language Pathologists
Speech-Language Pathology Assistants
Sports Medicine Physicians

Spotters, Dry Cleaning
Statement Clerks
Station Installers and Repairers, Telephone
Stationary Engineers
Statistical Assistants
Statisticians
Stevedores
Stock Clerks and Order Fillers
Stone Cutters and Carvers
Stone Sawyers
Stonemasons
Storage and Distribution Managers
Stringed Instrument Repairers and Tuners
Strippers
Structural Iron and Steel Workers
Structural Metal Fabricators and Fitters
Substance Abuse and Behavioral Disorder Counselors
Subway and Streetcar Operators
Supply Chain Managers*
Surgeons
Surgical Assistants
Surgical Technologists
Survey Researchers
Surveying and Mapping Technicians
Surveying Technicians
Surveyors
Sustainability Specialists
Switchboard Operators, Including Answering Service
Tailors, Dressmakers, and Custom Sewers
Talent Directors
Tank Car, Truck, and Ship Loaders
Tapers
Tax Examiners, Collectors, and Revenue Agents
Tax Preparers
Taxi Drivers and Chauffeurs
Teacher Assistants
Teachers and Instructors
Team Assemblers
Technical Directors--Managers
Technical Writers
Telecommunications Engineering Specialists
Telecommunications Equipment Installers and Repairers, Except Line Installers
Telecommunications Facility Examiners

Telecommunications Line Installers and Repairers
Telemarketers
Telephone Operators
Tellers
Terrazzo Workers and Finishers
Textile Bleaching and Dyeing Machine Operators and Tenders
Textile Cutting Machine Setters, Operators, and Tenders
Textile Knitting and Weaving Machine Setters, Operators, and Tenders
Textile Winding, Twisting, and Drawing Out Machine Setters, Operators, and Tenders
Textile, Apparel, and Furnishings Workers
Therapists
Tile and Marble Setters
Timing Device Assemblers, Adjusters, and Calibrators
Tire Builders
Tire Repairers and Changers
Title Examiners, Abstractors, and Searchers
Tool and Die Makers
Tool Grinders, Filers, and Sharpeners
Tour Guides and Escorts
Tour Guides and Escorts
Tractor-Trailer Truck Drivers
Traffic Technicians
Train Crew Members
Training and Development Manager
Training and Development Managers
Training and Development Specialists
Transformer Repairers
Transit and Railroad Police
Transportation Attendants
Transportation Engineers
Transportation Inspectors
Transportation Managers
Transportation Planners
Transportation Security Screeners
Transportation Vehicle, Equipment and Systems Inspectors
Transportation Workers
Transportation, Storage, and Distribution Managers
Travel Agents
Travel Clerks
Travel Guides

Treasurers, Controllers, and Chief Financial Officers
Tree Trimmers and Pruners
Truck Drivers, Heavy
Truck Drivers, Heavy and Tractor-Trailer
Truck Drivers, Light or Delivery Services
Tutors
Typesetting and Composing Machine Operators and Tenders
Umpires, Referees, and Other Sports Officials
Upholsterers
Urban and Regional Planners
Urologists
Ushers, Lobby Attendants, and Ticket Takers
Validation Engineers Valve and Regulator Repairers
Veterinarians
Veterinary Assistants and Laboratory Animal Caretakers
Veterinary Technologists and Technicians
Video Game Designers
Vocational Education Teachers
Waiters and Waitresses
Watch Repairers
Water and Liquid Waste Treatment Plant and System Operators
Water Resource Specialists
Water/Wastewater Engineers
Weatherization Installers and Technicians
Web Developers
Weighers, Measurers, Checkers, and Samplers, Recordkeeping
Welder-Fitters
Welders and Cutters
Welders, Cutters, and Welder Fitters
Welders, Cutters, Solderers, and Brazers
Welders, Production
Welding Machine Operators and Tenders
Welding Machine Setters and Set-Up Operators
Welding, Soldering, and Brazing Machine Setters, Operators, and Tenders
Welfare Eligibility Workers and Interviewers
Well and Core Drill Operators
Wellhead Pumpers
Wholesale and Retail Buyers, Except Farm Products
Wind Energy Engineers
Wind Energy Operations Managers
Wind Energy Project Managers
Wind Turbine Service Technicians
Woodworking Machine Operators and Tenders
Word Processors and Typists
Writers and Authors
Zoologists and Wildlife Biologists

DID YOU ADD YOUR INTERESTS TO YOUR CHART?

CHAPTER 2 – OH HECK NO!

Aspects you refuse to be part of
your everyday life.

In order to ensure the career you choose will be healthy for you long term, you need to think in negative terms - **for only 1 chapter**! People like different things. Obviously, people also dislike different things. It's important you dig into what you KNOW you don't want, to make sure your possible careers don't include them. Being a helicopter pilot, for example, can be a very rewarding career. Helicopters however are very expensive to operate. Most opportunities in the United States to be a pilot is for medivac type flights, which most are on call -nights and weekends. If you want a typical 9am-5pm, this career might be a difficult feat long term.

Keep in mind that **your limitations are self-imposed**. Don't discount something because you don't have enough practice in it or need to learn more about it. Write down things you absolutely don't want to deal with daily. Perhaps you KNOW you want 9-5; second and third shift therefore are out of the question.

I created this method while I lived in New Orleans Active Duty in the Marine Corps. I had always lived in "the sticks" and never had to deal with city traffic until then. I decided that no matter what I felt the perfect career would be for me, it would not include city driving. I have zero patience for bad or slow drivers! Anything including city (or large town, HA!) driving would not fit me.

In my hometown there is a large portion of the population utilizing government assistance. This results in a large group of people getting their paycheck on the first day of every month, which crowd the banks, Walmart, etc. This influx of people can make a usually easy trip take much longer and more stressful than any other day of the month! Are there situations you have dealt with that you can't see yourself dealing with day in and day out?

 **SPEND TIME KNOWING AND UNDERSTANDING YOUR LIMITS!**

WHAT DO YOU WANT TO STAY OUT OF YOUR LIFE?!

All definitions are provided by *Google* (www.Google.com) unless otherwise stated!

What are your pet peeves?
- "something that a particular person finds especially annoying."
"one of my biggest pet peeves is poor customer service"

_____

_____

What is your idea of a terrible day?
- Definition of terrible: "extremely unpleasant or disagreeable."
"the weather was terrible"

_____

_____

What makes you impatient?
- "having or showing a tendency to be quickly irritated or provoked."
"an impatient motorist blaring his horn"

_____

_____

What makes you angry?
- "a strong feeling of annoyance, displeasure, or hostility."
"the colonel's anger at his daughter's disobedience"

_____

_____

What annoys you?
- "irritate (someone); make (someone) a little angry."
"your cheerfulness has always annoyed me"

_____

_____

What makes you sad?

 - "feeling or showing sorrow; unhappy."
 "I was sad and subdued"

_____

_____

What makes you feel guilty?

 - "a feeling of having done wrong or failed in an obligation."
 "he remembered with sudden guilt the letter from his mother that he had not read"

_____

_____

What makes you feel fear?

 - "an unpleasant emotion caused by the belief that someone or something is
 dangerous, likely to cause pain, or a threat."
 "he is prey to irrational fears"

_____

_____

What makes you feel anxiety?

 - "a feeling of worry, nervousness, or unease, typically about an imminent
 event or something with an uncertain outcome."
 "he felt a surge of anxiety"

_____

_____

What makes you feel discouraged or in despair?

 - "the complete loss or absence of hope."
 "in despair, I exercise"

_____

_____

What makes you feel apathy?

> – "lack of interest, enthusiasm, or concern."
> "widespread apathy among students"

_____

_____

What makes you feel disappointed?

> – "fail to fulfill the hopes or expectations of (someone)."
> "I have no wish to disappoint everyone by postponing the visit"

_____

_____

What makes you feel frustrated?

> – "the feeling of being upset or annoyed, especially because of inability to change or achieve something."
> "I sometimes feel like screaming with frustration"

_____

_____

Is there anything else you really HATE?

> – "feel intense or passionate dislike for (someone)."
> "the boys hate each other"

_____

_____

 DID YOU UPDATE YOUR CHART?

CHAPTER 3 – HOBBIES

Whether you think you can get paid for them or not.

Now, what are hobbies? *Google* defines hobbies as **"an activity done regularly in one's leisure time for pleasure."** What do you already do for fun? Do you spend every second you have on Facebook creeping people that interest you? **Write it down,** maybe you'll find that you should be a talent scout because you can spot the "winners." Who knows? These should be the things that you do because you want to do it.

Being Active Duty away from home in New Orleans provided me an opportunity to really find out about myself. If I had free time, I was finding something wrong with whatever vehicle I had traded for that month so I could fix it. If there was nothing wrong with it, I would perform preventative maintenance, even if it was something that would probably never break anyways. I just liked tinkering – even if I wasn't confident in what I was doing. So, I wrote down mechanics as a hobby.

I spent so much of my free time on college, I also decided that I enjoyed the planning and research aspects of it. I liked planning and seeing those plans followed through. I still do. So, I wrote it down.

What do you do in your spare time for pleasure? What would you like to start doing? Circle the ones you have interested in and pick them apart. What is it you enjoy or would enjoy? Put these on your chart. You can use the thoughts you gain from them for both career ideas and hobbies that will stay just that; hobbies.

Move only one at a time.
<u>Contemplate</u> each hobby individually.
DO NOT PROGRESS UNTIL YOU ARE OUT OF THOUGHTS on each.

Wikipedia has a nice list of hobbies to help get your list started (some others added):

Indoor hobbies

3D printing
Acrobatics
Acting
Amateur radio
Animation
Aquascaping
Baking
Baton twirling
Beatboxing
Board/tabletop games
Book restoration
Cabaret
Calligraphy
Candle making
Coffee roasting
Collecting
Coloring
Computer programming
Cooking
Cosplaying
Couponing
Creative writing
Crocheting
Cross-stitch
Crossword puzzles
Cryptography
Dance
Digital arts
Do it yourself
Drama
Drawing
Electronics
Embroidery
Fantasy sports
Fashion
Fishkeeping
Flower arranging
Foreign language learning
Gaming (tabletop games and role-playing games)
Genealogy
Glassblowing
Graphic design
Gunsmithing
Herp keeping
Homebrewing
Hydroponics
Ice skating

Jewelry making
Jigsaw puzzles
Juggling
Knife making
Knitting
Kombucha brewing
Lace making
Lapidary
Leather crafting
Lego building
Lock Picking
Listening to music
Machining
Macrame
Magic
Metalworking
Model building
Model engineering
Needlepoint
Origami
Painting
Philately
Photography
Planning
Playing musical instruments
Poi
Pottery
Puzzles
Quilling
Quilting
Reading
Research
Robot combat
Scrapbooking
Sculpting
Sewing
Singing
Sketching
Soapmaking
Stand-up comedy
Table tennis
Taxidermy
Video game developing
Video gaming
Video editing
Watching movies
Watching television
Whittling
Wood carving
Woodworking
Worldbuilding
Writing

Yo-yoing
Yoga

Outdoor hobbies

Air sports
Archery
Astronomy
BASE jumping
Baseball
Basketball
Beekeeping
Bird watching
Blacksmithing
BMX
Board sports
Bodybuilding
Brazilian jiu-jitsu
Camping
Canoeing
Canyoning
Dowsing
Driving
Fishing
Flag football
Flying
Flying disc
Foraging
Freestyle football
Gardening
Geocaching
Ghost hunting
Gold prospecting
Graffiti
Handball
High-power rocketry
Hiking
Hooping
Horseback riding
Hunting
Inline skating
Jogging
Kayaking
Kite flying
Kitesurfing
LARPing
Letterboxing
Longboarding
Martial arts
Mechanics
Metal detecting
Motor sports
Mountain biking

Mountaineering
Mushroom hunting/
mycology
Netball
Nordic skating
Orienteering
Paintball
Parkour
Photography
Polo
Powerlifting
Rafting
Rappelling
Road biking
Rock climbing
Roller skating
Rugby
Running
Sailing
Sand art
Scouting
Scuba diving
Sculling or rowing
Shooting
Shopping
Skateboarding
Skiing
Skimboarding
Skydiving
Slacklining
Snowboarding
Stone skipping
Sun bathing
Surfing
Swimming
Taekwondo
Tai chi
Topiary
Travel
Urban exploration
Vacation
Vehicle restoration
Walking
Water sports

Collection hobbies indoors

Action figure
Antiquing
Art collecting
Book collecting
Cartophily (card
collecting)
Coin collecting
Comic book
collecting

Deltiology
(postcard
collecting)
Die-cast toy
Dolls
Element collecting
Fusilately
(phonecard
collecting)
Knife collecting
Lotology (lottery
ticket collecting)
Movie and movie
memorabilia
collecting
Perfume
Phillumeny
Rail transport
modelling
Record collecting
Shoes
Stamp collecting
Tea bag collecting
Video game
collecting
Vintage cars

Outdoors

Antiquities
Auto audiophilia
Flower collecting
and pressing
Fossil hunting
Insect collecting
Magnet fishing
Metal detecting
Mineral collecting
Rock balancing
Sea glass
collecting
Seashell collecting
Stone collecting

Competitive hobbies indoors

Animal fancy
Badminton
Baton twirling
Billiards
Bowling
Boxing
Bridge
Cheerleading
Chess

Color guard
Curling
Dancing
Darts
Debate
Eating
ESports
Fencing
Gymnastics
Ice skating
Kabaddi
Laser tag
Longboarding
Mahjong
Marbles
Martial arts
Poker
Shogi
Slot car racing
Speedcubing
Sport stacking
Table football
Volleyball
Weightlifting
Wrestling

Outdoors

Airsoft
American football
Archery
Association
football
Astrology
Australian rules
football
Auto racing
Baseball
Beach volleyball
Breakdancing
Climbing
Cricket
Cycling
Disc golf
Dog sport
Equestrianism
Exhibition drill
Field hockey
Figure skating
Fishing
Footbag
Golfing
Handball
Horseback riding
Ice hockey
Judo
Jukskei
Kart racing

Knife throwing
Lacrosse
Longboarding
Marching band
Model aircraft
Racquetball
Radio-controlled
car racing
Roller derby
Rugby league
football
Sculling or rowing
Shooting sport
Skateboarding
Speed skating
Squash
Surfing
Swimming
Table tennis
Tennis
Tennis polo

Tether car
Tour skating
Triathlon
Ultimate frisbee
Volleyball
Water polo

Observation hobbies indoors

Fishkeeping
Learning
Meditation
Microscopy
Reading
Shortwave listening
Audio/Videophilia

Outdoors

Aircraft spotting
Amateur
astronomy
Birdwatching
Bus spotting
Geocaching
Gongoozling
Herping
Hiking/back
packing
Meteorology
Photography
Satellite watching
Trainspotting
Traveling
Whale watching

DID YOU UPDATE YOUR CHART?

CHAPTER 4 – EXPERIENCE AND BACKGROUND

Work history, knowledge, abilities and skills.

What have you done in the past? Worked at a gas station making pizzas and checking out customers? Jot down customer service. Waiting tables? Jot down customer service and sales (hey, dessert is an upsell for a larger check and tip!). Time to make a resume if you don't have one!

These are the definitions (provided by *Google*) you need for the following exercises:

Life Event - A very important event in someone's life.
> "Today is the most important day (event) of my life."
> Such as: marriage, child birth, death of a family member, moving

Gained Experience - Practical contact with and observation of facts or events.
> "He had already learned his lesson by painful experience."
> Such as: communication, self-management, self-control, patience

Work History (employment history) – A detailed report of all the jobs you have held.
> "I have worked in numerous fields."
> Such as: past jobs, volunteering, commendations, awards

Knowledge – Facts, information and skills acquired by experience or education.
> "A thirst for knowledge;" the practical understanding of a subject.
> Such as: having the ability to find a location, remembering details about an event

> ***Note** – Abilities and Skills can blend together. That's ok!
> Just contemplate each event.

Ability - Possession of the means or to do something; naturally gifted.
> "The manager had lost his ability to motivate the players."
> Such as: decision making, time management, self-motivation, leadership, Adaptability, teamwork, creativity, compassion, courtesy, courage, integrity, confidence

Skill - The ability to do something well; learned expertise or a fine-tuned ability.
> "Difficult work, taking great skill."
> Such as: knowing how to make a pizza, how to thread a needle or search the internet

The following template is partially provided by wikiHow, *"a wiki building the world's largest, highest quality how-to manual. Please edit this article and find author credits at wikiHow.com. Content on wikiHow can be shared under a Creative Commons License."*

Even more help can be found at: https://www.wikiHow.com/Make-a-Resume.

 DO YOUR BEST TO CREATE YOUR RESUME AND THEN MOVE ON TO THE NEXT EXERCISE.
YOU WILL COME BACK TO REVISIT THIS RESUME AFTER MORE REFLECTION.

NAME _____

ADDRESS _____

PHONE NUMBER _____

PROFESSIONAL EMAIL ADDRESS _____
(GET A NEW ONE IF YOU HAVE TO! FIRSTNAME.LASTNAME@GOOGLE.COM)

OBJECTIVE (vow)

_____

EDUCATION

Degrees _____

Certificates _____

TECHNICAL SKILLS (THAT RELATE TO WORK ENVIRONMENTS)

Examples: Microsoft Office, Internet searches, troubleshooting computer issues, verbal and written communication skills, words you can type per minute etc.

_____

_____

PROFESSIONAL SKILLS (THAT RELATE TO WORK ENVIRONMENTS)

Examples: Experience in culinary arts, childcare, exercise equipment maintenance, etc.

_____

_____

EMPLOYMENT HISTORY (INCLUDE ANY VOLUNTEER WORK)

_____

_____

HOBBIES AND INTERESTS (THAT RELATE TO WORK ENVIRONMENTS)

_____

_____

My experience and background came mostly from my Active Duty time in the Marine Corps and college. I majored in business, knowing that wherever I was going work or what I was going to do, it would be some sort of business. I was still at this point interested in becoming a police officer, which is benefited with a college degree – in almost any major. Dealing with people can be its own business. If you don't believe me, read the *Little Green Book of Getting Your Way by* Jeffrey Gitomer!

My sales experience came from USMC Recruiter Aide work and my background came from personal "deals" my whole life of buying/selling/upgrading vehicles. My management experience also came from the USMC and as being Sergeant of Arms in my High School VoTech Criminal Justice Class. I also grew immensely in the USMC with two of my MOS's - Marksmanship Coach and Rifleman. From becoming very attentive to details where a single breath could change your shot to perseverance in difficult days. There are always lessons from the experiences you have had.

While Active Duty, I also spent time as an Administration Clerk in a setting where huge growth was occurring. It was very important to set up daily written procedures, which I thrived at creating and documenting. This is how I came up with organizing and planning, but also because I am a very detail-orientated person that must have all my personal belongings organized and my every day planned. I carry around a to-do list every day in my pocket, and I always have!

"Do not pray for an easy life, pray for the strength to endure a difficult one" - Bruce Lee

---

Some events or experiences may jog difficult memories or situations. These things do not necessarily need to go under the "No" column if they are something you can train, grow and learn from. Perhaps it was difficult but exciting! Sometimes the most challenging things in life bring us the most joy.

* * *

Time for some reflection on your side. Think about and write down 20 life events that you have had, preferably that have brought you joy or simply pop into your mind as events. Getting a Christmas tree as a child, going to the mall with your friends, helping your neighbor carry groceries etc. Then break them down as listed.

READ THE NEXT STOP SIGN!!!

YOU MUST DO THIS IN 3 STEPS!

DO NOT DO A WHOLE EVENT AT ONCE!

(1) Write down your 20 events
(2) Read definition for single category & reflect for each event separately
(3) THEN move to the next category for each event separately

Life Event	Gained Experience	Work History
1_____

Knowledge	Ability	Skill

Life Event	Gained Experience	Work History
2_____

Knowledge	Ability	Skill

Life Event	Gained Experience	Work History
3_____

Knowledge	Ability	Skill

Life Event	Gained Experience	Work History
4_____

Knowledge	Ability	Skill

Life Event	Gained Experience	Work History
5_____

Knowledge	Ability	Skill

Life Event	Gained Experience	Work History
6_____

Knowledge	Ability	Skill

Life Event	Gained Experience	Work History
7_____

Knowledge	Ability	Skill

Life Event   Gained Experience   Work History

8_____

Knowledge   Ability   Skill

_____

Life Event   Gained Experience   Work History

9_____

Knowledge   Ability   Skill

_____

Life Event   Gained Experience   Work History

10_____

Knowledge   Ability   Skill

_____

Life Event   Gained Experience   Work History

11_____

Knowledge   Ability   Skill

_____

Life Event   Gained Experience   Work History

12_____

Knowledge   Ability   Skill

_____

Life Event   Gained Experience   Work History

13_____

Knowledge   Ability   Skill

_____

Life Event   Gained Experience   Work History

14_____

Knowledge   Ability   Skill

_____

Life Event	Gained Experience	Work History
15		
Knowledge	Ability	Skill

Life Event	Gained Experience	Work History
16		
Knowledge	Ability	Skill

Life Event	Gained Experience	Work History
17		
Knowledge	Ability	Skill

Life Event	Gained Experience	Work History
18		
Knowledge	Ability	Skill

Life Event	Gained Experience	Work History
19		
Knowledge	Ability	Skill

Life Event	Gained Experience	Work History
20		
Knowledge	Ability	Skill

REVISIT YOUR RESUME AND UPDATE IT!
&
UPDATE YOUR CHART!

 **Contemplate the events and the aspects you have written down.**

What have you written down more than once?

Reoccurrences can help point out aspects of your life that have opportunity to help in your career decision. Perhaps you have extensive practice in a certain skill or gravitate to a certain type of work. Looking into your past can help point you in the right direction for the future. Take your time! **Even if something only came up once but it is important to you, write it down!**

Ten noticed reoccurrences or importances:

1 _____

2 _____

3 _____

4 _____

5 _____

6 _____

7 _____

8 _____

9 _____

10 _____

* * *

PERSONAL MISSION STATEMENT

These events that brought you joy and contributed to the well-being of others may show a history of your personality that may offer career ideas. How can these reoccurrences be used to help others? To find out, let's create 2 mission statements using these reoccurrences. A business' mission statement is designed to guide that business, to keep them on track daily as they grow. Why should we not have our own personal mission statements?

Imagine being given an award by the President at the age of 90 for one of the 10 noticed reoccurrences or some of the life events you wrote down. You have spent your entire life dedicated to whatever seems the most important one to you. What award are you getting?

A personal mission statement is like your Ikigai, the reason why you get out of bed every morning, which is usually positive and to the benefit of others. Take your vow and see if it can be remolded with this model. **What is YOUR mission in life?**

In Google's words, a mission statement is: "a formal summary of the aims and values of a company, organization, or individual."

Consider some business examples:

- "To conserve and restore natural ecosystems, focusing on birds, other wildlife, and their habitats for the benefit of humanity and the earth's biological diversity." - Audubon
- "To provide better care of the sick, investigation into their problems, and further education of those who serve." – Cleveland Clinic
- "To work in partnership with member stations to create a more informed public – one challenged and invigorated by a deeper understanding and appreciation of events, ideas and cultures." - NPR
- "To create content that educates, informs and inspires." – Public Broadcasting System (PBS)
- "Spreading Ideas." – Technology, Entertainment, Design (TED)
- "Celebrating Animals, Confronting Cruelty" – The Humane Society
- "The USO strengthens America's military service members by keeping them connected to family, home, and country, throughout their service to the nation." – USO

Consider some personal examples from prominent business people:

- "To serve as a leader, live a balanced life, and apply ethical principles to make a significant difference." - Denise Morrison, Campbell Soup Company
- "To use my gifts of intelligence, charisma, and serial optimism to cultivate the self-worth and net-worth of women around the world." - Amanda Steinberg, Dailyworth.com
- "To be a teacher. And to be known for inspiring my students to be more than they thought they could be." - Oprah Winfrey, OWN
- "To have fun in my journey through life and learn from my mistakes." - Richard Branson, The Virgin Group
- "To live life with integrity and empathy and be a positive force in the lives of others." - Amy Ziari, "Pasta"

When drafting your own, consider your personal goals for yourself. What type of person do you want to be? What image do you want to portray? How do you want to be remembered? Think in terms of your vow, but in a more generic, lifelong overview.

YOUR PERSONAL MISSION STATEMENT :

_____

_____

    DID YOU UPDATE YOUR CHART

CHAPTER 5 – ENVIRONMENT

Who, What, When, Where, Why, How

Think about the environment you want to live in 5 + days a week, 40 + hours per day. Would you enjoy being a prison guard at a maximum-security prison in an honorable position of control? Or would you feel being surrounded by the world's worst criminals would grind down your personality? Would you enjoy being a sailboat instructor at a sandy beach vacation resort with wind whipping through your hair and sun beating on your brow? Or is that too far from home and you can't swim! Indoors or outdoors; think of the overall daily routine you prefer.

I knew my personality type was GO-GO-GO so I needed an environment that provided change and optional challenges. Optional because I like to work at my own speed demon pace most times but slow and methodical in certain circumstances or solving certain problems. I also knew from my time in the USMC that I wanted limited rules; an open environment where I could choose my own circumstances, with promotion resulting directly from accomplishments, not relying upon a board or some sort of social standing once achieving a certain rank. Think of your own ideal environment designed for you to thrive.

PUT THOUGHT INTO IT!
LOOK AT EACH CAREER SEPERATELY THAT YOU ARE CONSIDERING.
YOU WILL ONLY GET OUT OF THIS WHAT YOU PUT INTO IT!

Who - People you do/don't want to work with? Work for? Provide services for?
Who is on the team? Who benefits? Break down "Who" in your own terms.
Think in terms of your vow and compare to your chart.
"what or which person or people"

_____

_____

What – Certain things you do/don't want in your environment.
Think in terms of your vow and compare to your chart.
"asking for information specifying something"

_____

_____

When – Are there certain hours or shifts you prefer? Dislike? Refuse? Certain seasons?
Certain days of the week you do/don't want to work?
Think in terms of your vow and compare to your chart.
"in what circumstances"

_____

_____

Where – Geographical locations you do/don't like? Close to home or not?
Inside/outside? Office, shop, home, plant, etc? Relocate? Travel frequently?
Think in terms of your vow and compare to your chart.
"in or to what place or position"

_____

_____

Why – Why will you do it? Specifically relating to your environment. To help others?
Serving what purpose?
Think in terms of your vow and compare to your chart.
"for what reason or purpose"

_____

_____

How – What means will the work be done? Manually? With equipment or technology?
Quickly/slowly? Up/down? Backwards/Forwards?
Think in terms of your vow and compare to your chart.
"In what way or manner; by what means"

_____

_____

IMMUTABLE LAWS

On my most recent trip my wife and I had breakfast at a local restaurant in Flagstaff, AZ. Breakfast was awesome! We walked out after eating and found a homeless man sitting in front of our rental van. I expected an awkward plead for money. Instead, he was a super nice guy, first asking if we were from NH where our rental van was from. We spoke for a moment, when he told us he was just sitting there to "watch over our van." My wife and I looked at each other while lifting our brows.

"Your side door is open," he said. "HuhhHH??" we walked around the van to see that the power door button must have been pressed in my pocket when we went inside and sat down. He assured us numerous times that he didn't take anything. Between laptops and equipment there were thousands of dollars of belongings in the van while we traveled the country! Once we realized he really did watch the van as our guardian angel; all he asked for was some breakfast. We at this point forgot we even had the leftovers that he was talking about! I told him to sit tight for just a minute, and pointed at a gas station, "I'm going to the ATM and getting you some cash, THANK YOU!!"

We went, came back and gave him cash. "It is much better in life to take care of others, not take from them" he said. He saluted me when we backed out of the parking lot. What an awesome experience and one to remember not to judge others. This man easily could have walked away with things (including the only copy I had of this book!) that meant a lot to us, but instead, he acted as our guardian angel. Thank you, random kind man! He obviously lives by "Immutable Laws."

When creating my first few business plans, I pinpointed "Immutable Laws" explained by one of my favorites, Mike Michalowicz. Mike explains these as:

"The rules of our lives. They define you. They define your business. They are a blend of ethics, core values and self-assigned law, all wrapped up into one. They are the rules we have defined for ourselves, almost subconsciously, on what is right and what is wrong. What is acceptable and what is not. What makes you happy, and what doesn't. They are with you for life and they barely ever change."

Mike explains these laws like the devil and angel on your shoulders – punishing you when you break them and patting you on the back when you follow them. They keep you on the straight and narrow from an unconscious level and our goal is to become aware of them. I have a feeling that throughout other exercises in this guide these should come forward reasonably easily. Think of the positive or negative events you have written down, your vow, and look at your chart to make them conscious and compare them with your possible careers.

Mike gives examples of these Immutable Laws on his website, along with a slew of other fantastic information: https://www.mikemichalowicz.com. Check out a partial list of his premade *Smorgasbord of Immutable Laws* he gives as an example to get your own Immutable Law juices flowing:

- **Dive Deep Enough to Touch Bottom** – When working with a client, we dive the deepest possible to understand the challenges they face. Only once we touch bottom are we in position to fully help them.

- **Carpe Diem** – Live in the moment and live for the day.

- **Positivity or Death** – A positive or a negative can be taken from every situation. It is a conscious choice. While everything may not go our way all the time and we won't always be happy campers, we will consciously always choose to be positive. Our positivity guides us to opportunities.

- **Turn the Turtles** – A struggling customer is like a turtle on its back. It is always our responsibility to put them back on their feet.

- **Blood Money** – We treat money like blood. Without it our business would die. We treat it with the utmost care and respect.

- **Get Rich Right** – Wealth is a vehicle for doing more good for ourselves, our community and our world.

- **Give to Give** – "Give to get" implies that you have a hidden agenda. We believe in giving for the joy of giving. Getting is irrelevant.

- **The Elvis Pelvis** – Pushing the limits on the industry norms is a good thing. We shake it up, like Elvis did. We just skip the "Fat Elvis" part.

These were mine!

Enjoyment is Contagious –

This organization is driven by the fact that customer service is not a marketing plan, but a way of life. It will be reflected in our everyday working habits and backed by our employee-friendly, family environment. We will exploit fun, enjoyment and laughter at no one else's expense and treat our colleagues, suppliers, customers and all others respectfully through our common good values.

Reinventing Quality –

We will force dictionaries to enhance their definitions of quality and force competitors to look to us as the automotive detailing and accessory professionals. We will be overall aware of our goals and achieve them through a common love of a rewarding establishment. Management vows to give employees the tools necessary to fulfill our responsibilities with ease and create a comfortable environment that customers will have their requests before requested.

Blood Money –

Financial stability and sustainable profit growth is the blood of all businesses, and we will represent such accordingly throughout constant control and monitoring. We will employ creative, innovative, redefining cost-cutting methods and employee high-profit, low risk methods in order to sustain long term financial health.

 SPEND SOME TIME CONSIDERING YOUR OWN IMMUTABLE LAWS.

MOLD THEM FROM THE OTHER "PROJECTS" IN THIS GUIDE.

MAKE SURE YOU UPDATE YOUR CHART!

Your Immutable Laws:

_____

_____

_____

_____

_____

_____

CHAPTER 6 – WANT

What we would like to have
but can live without.

Google defines a want as to *"have a desire to possess or do (something); wish for."* I would define a want as something that we would like to have, would be nice to have, but we can live without. For this guide, it differs from a requirement:

<u>**A WANT** can be overlooked –</u>

<u>It is something that would be nice to have, but we can live without.</u>

<u>**A REQUIREMENT** (or need) is set in stone</u>

<u>It is necessary in our lives; there is no way for us to live without it.</u>

We all want to be a millionaire and the most successful person in the world! Our goals however should force us to strive for them and should be **just out of our grasp but attainable**. Not something so far out of the realm of a possibility it becomes a daydream that does us no good or offers us no motivation. You decide your dream. I had a picture of a private island at my desk I hoped to own someday! My wants changed or I would still have that picture up!

"Two people could argue for hours about whether a given product or service is a need. Obviously, circumstance and frames of reference are important in this discussion. What one person needs, another person wants. Quite simply, the economic definition of a **need is something needed to survive**. In economics, the idea of survival is real, meaning someone would die without their needs being met. This includes things like food, water and shelter. A want, in economics, is one step up in the order from needs and is simply something that people desire to have, that they may, or may not, be able to obtain."
- The Difference Between Wants vs. Needs in Economics by Dr. Douglas Hawks

---

My wants and motivation were self-fulfillment and success. Success specifically being financial stability to the point of having reasonable, expendable income for "toys" or the ability to attain some of my daily wants. Self-fulfillment to me simply meant attaining happiness in my career. Being happy with what I was doing. These two things were essentially my watered-down version of Maslow's highest level of motivation in his Hierarchy of Needs; or *"What a man can be, he must be."* – Earl Nightingale.

Looking at the well-known *Maslow's Hierarchy of Needs* can greatly help with your search for the career you deserve. Consider each portion of his triangle for possible additions to your chart in the aspect of WANTS (if you come up with needs, write them down too!):

Physiological wants - Think of food, water, sleep & shelter in an "unnecessary" fashion

_____

_____

Safety wants - Not only physical safety but financial & emotional

_____

_____

Social wants – Not only friendship and family but intimacy with another

_____

_____

Self-esteem – Personal satisfaction regarding standing or respect received from others

_____

_____

Self-actualization – Utilizing one's skills, abilities and talents

_____

_____

HAVE YOU BEEN UPDATING YOUR CHART?

SALARY WANT VS. REQUIRED

This is a great time to figure out what type of salary you would like to have! Be reasonable but comfortable. Anyone would LIKE to have a $150,000 salary every year; but what number would you be comfortable at?

BE REASONABLE

Inflating your required salary to a sky-high number is going to negate several of the careers you have chosen. Everyone daydreams or scrolls through social media looking at pictures of rich celebrities that have huge extravagant mansions, yachts, Ferraris and Lamborghinis but let's be real —only a very small portion of us will have these things. Do not exaggerate to an unreasonable number.

BE COMFORTABLE

Figure out your approximate monthly expenses and budget for hobbies, free time and vacations. Do not round down on utility bills in hopes you will cut costs. Do not hope or plan that your 10-year-old car will last another 15 years and you will not need another. Make sure your salary is going to be high enough to cover unforeseen expenses and give you a comfortable life.

FRUGAL FINATIC

Frugal Finatic provides information on saving, making and budgeting your money on www.frugalfinatic.com. They created the following worksheet in which you should go through and calculate your Budget Amount for each Expenses and Savings item, and total at the end. Use this total, add to your Savings items if you underestimated a fair value, and add 10% for any bills you may have forgotten. This is your approximate salary requirement. Think of the Budget Amount as your current salary requirement, and the Actual Amount as your planned salary requirement.

Here is a quick run-down provided by www.FrugalFanatic.com; just **don't forget to take income taxes into account, and if you haven't paid these bills yet in life ask your parents or another source that have the lifestyle you want.**

Monthly Budget

Frugal Fanatic

Items	Budget Amount	Actual Amount	Difference	Notes
INCOME				
Income Total				
Other Income				
EXPENSES				
Mortgage/Rent				
Household Maintenance				
Taxes				
Insurance				
Electricity				
Water				
Sewage				
Gas				
Phone				
Trash				
Cable				
Cell Phone				
Groceries				
Entertainment				
Charity/Donations				
Fuel				
Auto Insurance				
Car Payment				
Child Care				
Credit Cards/Debt				
Loans				
Child Support				
Clothing				
SAVINGS				
Retirement				
College				
Basic/Other				
TOTALS				

Total Income - Total Expenses $_____

Ganley, Addi. "Monthly Budget" chart. Frugal Fanatic. www.frugalfanatic.com. Accessed 22 Apr. 2019.

57 Things Other People Want From Life – by Mindy Tyson McHorse

Mindy poses a great question in her article: *"If a genie suddenly appeared and offered to grant you a single wish, what would you say?"* She created this list of regular wants in life that should get some "juices flowing" for you on what you might spend your income on (minor changes made). Take each idea individually into consideration and come up with your own! How do these wants relate to finding the career you deserve? Write them down and reflect

Material Things
Big house
Nice car
Fashionable clothes
Plenty of money for dining out
A budget for luxury travel
Thin friends
An attractive spouse

Self-Confidence Things
To neither look nor feel fat
To eat whatever and not gain weight
To hold your own in a political conversation
To learn to dance without looking stupid
To be attractive as you age
To be the life of the party, at least once
To know what you want and have the confidence to go after it

Adventurous Things
Visit every continent
Speak a foreign language
Learn how to take professional photographs
Go cliff diving or skydiving
Live in a beautiful place
Volunteer in a disaster zone
Go to a major sports championship
Pilot a plane
Spend New Year's in NYC

Spiritual/Emotional Things

Have at least one true best friend
Feel relief from social judgment
Reconcile with an enemy
Be remembered in a positive way after death
Know that you made a difference in someone else's life
Feel important to others
Know yourself and feel centered
Live each day without regret
Quiet self-limiting thoughts

Career-Related Things

Reach a fabled level of success
A positive work/life balance
Feel as capable as others think you are
Be productive with each minute of the day
Be recognized as talented or even brilliant
Pursue your calling while supporting your family financially
Publish a book
To financially care for aging parents
Write a screenplay that turns into a movie

Lifestyle Things

Start every morning with a leisurely cup of coffee
Travel the country in an RV
Have many children and grandchildren
Stay married to the same person
Find meaningful work
Find the best piece of pie, ever
Give your dog a happy life

Health Things

Grow old without losing your mind or control of your body
Recover from a painful or debilitating disease
Not die from a painful or debilitating disease
Have plenty of energy to enjoy each day
Age gracefully, without wrinkles or going bald
Find a way to enjoy exercise
Finish a marathon or an ironman triathlon

DID YOU UPDATE YOUR CHART?

McHorse, Mindy Tyson. "57 Things Other People Want From Life." August 2011. American

Writers & Artists Inc. https://www.awai.com/2011/08/57-things-other-people-want-from-life/.

CHAPTER 7 – REQUIREMENTS

Things that unequivocally **<u>MUST</u>** be included.

Requirements are more than a want. They unequivocally MUST be included in the career you deserve. What do you HAVE TO HAVE? Perhaps you want a certain type of life with a flexible schedule, or maybe you're a workaholic and need the ability to take overtime for more cash. Remember, for this guide:

<u>A WANT</u> can be overlooked –

<u>It is something that would be nice to have, but we can live without</u>.

<u>A REQUIREMENT</u> (or need) is set in stone

<u>It is necessary in our lives; there is no way for us to live without it.</u>

My wife hates when I say it, but even if you were born rich, **you've got to pay to play**! Make sure your requirements do not turn into a "daydream." Keep them high enough to strive for, a little bit out of reach but close enough to reasonability you can make them happen. Expect that for most careers to be rewarding you need to "climb the ladder."

What <u>MUST</u> I have out of life?

_____

_____

What will that require out of a career?

_____

_____

What will that require out of me?

_____

_____

What did I write down as a want, that really may be a requirement?

_____

_____

Take another look at *Maslow's Hierarchy of Needs* and consider each portion of his triangle for possible additions to your chart in terms of REQUIREMENTS (needs):

Physiological needs – Think food, water, sleep & shelter

_____

_____

Safety needs – Not only physical safety but financial & emotional

_____

_____

Social belonging – Not only friendship and family but intimacy with another

_____

_____

Self-esteem – Personal satisfaction regarding standing or respect received from others

_____

_____

Self-actualization – Utilizing one's abilities and talents

_____

_____

RETIREMENT

I knew I wanted a career that would offer me some sort of retirement. Whether it be IRA/401K or my own personal savings and investments, I knew I didn't want to work forever and wanted to plan ahead. I also knew that some of my options, like becoming a police officer would be more conducive to retirement younger in life.

What do you require out of your career to prepare you for retirement?

_____

_____

ADVANCEMENT

I wanted to have a certain type of lifestyle which required me to make at least $70,000 per year within 5 years. I knew that many careers require "stepping-stones" and making this amount right off the bat might not be feasible. Advancement therefore was a requirement – the ability for me to grow in a position and strive to improve myself and the company.

Is there certain advancement you are looking for?

_____

_____

Is there a "stepping-stone" you MUST **start** at?

_____

_____

Is there a "stepping-stone" you MUST **arrive** at in a certain time period?

_____

_____

VACATION TIME

Time off may not have been possible with all of my choices right off the bat, but it did need to be possible with advancement so I could travel. I wanted to live in my hometown so I would not have accepted a career that REQUIRED me to travel, just the opportunity to do so while living where I grew up.

Do you HAVE to have a certain amount of vacation or sick time? After how long?

_____

_____

WORK LIFE BALANCE / LENIENCY

Are you a typical 9am – 5pm worker, or do you need a flexible schedule? Some careers allow easy arrangements for other programs and practices, while some are "all work and no play." What type of personal, family or social activities do you have that may interfere with a typical schedule? Do you have a young child always at the doctor or are you available to work whenever necessary to get the job done?

 WHAT HAVE YOU MADE A REQUIREMENT THAT REALLY IS A WANT? STOP AND STARE AT YOUR CHART FOR A WHILE. THE LONGER YOU THE BETTER – THOUGHTS AND IDEAS WILL COME TO YOU

 DID YOU UPDATE YOUR CHART?

CHAPTER 8 – ON THE SIDE

Careers we may like to pursue

on a part time basis.

Perhaps you have added careers into your Career Possibilities column that you can't see yourself doing full time, or they wouldn't provide substantial hours, pay, or other requirements. Could any be joined together? Perhaps two halves make a whole? If not but they mean enough to you that you want them to be a part of your life, they should! Consider them as a means of volunteering or as a hobby and move them to that category. I call this "cleaning out the riff raff" – BUT **DO NOT ERASE ANYTHING FROM YOUR CHART**! Just move it if necessary.

First, go to your chart, and look online for the salary range of each career you have written down. If a career may start at $30,000 per year but has the potential to be $50,000 in 5 years, then write it down! You can now see which careers meet your required salary, and which careers may possibly be joined together (i.e. 2 part time to make a full-time career). If any exist, move them together into this category. An example would be owning a small car lot for part time work, and a small lawn care company at the same time.

 UPDATE YOUR LIST OF CAREER POSSIBILITIES WITH THEIR SALARIES

Career Possibility: (fitting your salary requirement)	Part Time Possibility?	Volunteer Possibility?	Hobby?
_____	Y / N	Y / N	Y / N
_____	Y / N	Y / N	Y / N
_____	Y / N	Y / N	Y / N
_____	Y / N	Y / N	Y / N
_____	Y / N	Y / N	Y / N

Career Possibility: (fitting your salary requirement)	Part Time Possibility?	Volunteer Possibility?	Hobby?
_____	Y / N	Y / N	Y / N
_____	Y / N	Y / N	Y / N
_____	Y / N	Y / N	Y / N
_____	Y / N	Y / N	Y / N
_____	Y / N	Y / N	Y / N
_____	Y / N	Y / N	Y / N
_____	Y / N	Y / N	Y / N
_____	Y / N	Y / N	Y / N
_____	Y / N	Y / N	Y / N
_____	Y / N	Y / N	Y / N
_____	Y / N	Y / N	Y / N
_____	Y / N	Y / N	Y / N
_____	Y / N	Y / N	Y / N
_____	Y / N	Y / N	Y / N
_____	Y / N	Y / N	Y / N

CAN SOME BE PUT TOGETHER?

DID YOU UPDATE YOUR CHART?

CHAPTER 9 – CAREER POSSIBILITIES

Careers worth "testing."

Now that you have created this list of possible life-long careers, it's time to test them against the categories you have filled. Take each career individually and **"rate" or "test"** it against the categories found on your chart. You will later rate them against each other.

If you find yourself **"manipulating"** or modifying ratings of a certain career, take the time to understand why. Do you have specific reasons you like or dislike that option? Annotate it and modify as you feel necessary! This is **your future** and **your options**. Rate 5 points for each positive aspects of each category for that career.

Example - If one of your No's is "not working nights" and a career possibility is day shift only, rate it 5 points. Rate 0 points for not applicable or neither positive or negative, or -5 points for negative aspects (that career includes working nights).

If - you feel one aspect is more or less important, **use your own scales**. 1 point, 10 points, rate the importance YOU feel each rate. <u>Leave the # category until last to rate careers by most to least total points.</u>

THIS MAY BE THE MOST IMPORTANT PART!

TAKE YOUR TIME!

Career Possibility:	No's	Environment	Want	Requirements	Salary	Total	#
[---------------- NUMBERS ONLY!! ------------------]							
_____	___	___	___	___	___	___	___
_____	___	___	___	___	___	___	___
_____	___	___	___	___	___	___	___
_____	___	___	___	___	___	___	___
_____	___	___	___	___	___	___	___

Career Possibility:	No's	Environment	Want	Requirements	Salary	Total	#
————————	—	—	—	—	—	—	—
————————	—	—	—	—	—	—	—
————————	—	—	—	—	—	—	—
————————	—	—	—	—	—	—	—
————————	—	—	—	—	—	—	—
————————	—	—	—	—	—	—	—
————————	—	—	—	—	—	—	—
————————	—	—	—	—	—	—	—
————————	—	—	—	—	—	—	—

How do you feel? Are you happy with the outcome? Do you have feelings that one career should be above or below another? Why? Contemplate, consider and reflect. Take the amount of time you need to ensure you feel happy with the results.

You now have not only figured out your choice career you deserve, but have a Plan B, C and maybe more. You however MUST tell yourself that your top choice is your only choice. Whatever the career is you have chosen as number 1; YOU have decided this. Do not get overwhelmed that maybe this choice requires more schooling, training, or personal change. **YOU** feel it is your best option; **YOU** have rated these sacrifices as less important than your overall long-term happiness with the career **YOU** deserve.

DID YOU UPDATE YOUR CHART?

YOU WILL WANT TO LOOK BACK TO IT IN THE FUTURE TO ENSURE YOURSELF THE DECISION YOU ARE MAKING IS THE CORRECT DECISION!

DO NOT ERASE ANYTHING!

CHAPTER 10 – MOVING FORWARD

What do you do now?

Moving forward is the hardest part! Even with every "i" dotted, every "t" crossed, and every box checked, it takes self-motivation to get out there and make things happen. You have made it this far! You can do it! Consider more of my favorite quotes while moving forward:

"Confidence is everything."- Unknown Author

In my opinion, the single most important secret to success is confidence. You must believe in yourself to succeed – and you will. If you believe you will fail, well, then you will probably do that instead. Low confidence will result in a failure to finish, but confidence "in check" (not overconfident) will result in your ability to finish anything.

"~~Life~~ is a business.
Business is business." – Kyle Crandall

Don't take life too seriously. But remember, business is business. There may be things you don't want to do and must – that's life! (I know, full circle, right?)

"Never burn a bridge." – Donna Crandall, my mother

I have found that every single relationship you make in life will also come around in "full circle." Think of it like karma. Every person you right, will return you a right. Every person you wrong, will return you a wrong.

"People do what you inspect, not what you expect."- Louis V. Gerstner, Jr.

No matter what you do or how you do it, find ways to keep yourself and others accountable. Otherwise, what was the point?

"You can't fix stupid" – Ron White

If something makes absolutely no sense at all but there is nothing you can do about it – either live with it or find another way.

"Inspiration comes from the need to succeed for self-sustainment, which is increased by the possibility to fail and requires a positive mental attitude." – Kyle Crandall

Being inspired is almost as important as being confident. To be inspired we must be driven to accomplish our goals and possess the ability to stay positive.

"The customer is always the customer." – Unknown

Even if you don't agree with a customer's stance, remember it is their business that keeps your world going around. Meet everyone with respect but **it is ok** to require the same in return. The same goes in life relationships.

"A job is only a short-term solution to a long-term problem." - Robert Toru Kiyosaki

A job is a paycheck. A way to pay the bills while going after your goals. A career is so much more. It is a rewarding activity that doesn't feel like work every day.

Now use this information that you have worked so hard to attain! Be proud of yourself and keep the positive mental attitude you needed while working on this quest! You have made huge strides towards the career you deserve, and the next steps belong to you. Make a precise plan with weekly, monthly and even yearly goals to attain this career. Rework your vow/promise to yourself to ensure you will not falter on your journey to a better you and do not rest until you make it so! Turn your vow card into a "goals card" that you carry with you every day, as a frequent reminder of your goals to make your dreams reality.

When moving forward remember that it's unlikely we narrowed down our specific goals to a "T". As an example, I knew my number 1 chosen career was to own my own business. I am glad I kept this goal broad, because I struggled through multiple business plans and failed business acquisition attempts before finding the right fit. Plan for this. Do not give up too quickly on any one idea and remember it may take multiple tries to find the perfect fit for your long-term future.

* * *

Planning Adulting - Goals Basics

(1) **Specific** - Set your goals with specifics... Clearly define them.

(2) **Measurable** - Make your goals measurable. Define timelines you can hold yourself to.

(3) **Reasonability** – Make your goals a stretch to strive for, but not for an Olympic athlete.

(4) **Relevant** – Keep your goals in check with your vow and chosen career. Keep these goals away from other things you are trying to attain (working out, getting the new iPhone, etc)

(5) **You are what you think about** – Remind yourself of what you have achieved already. Make a vow card, set aside times to work on these goals. Make them make a new you.

CAREER 1 – PLAN A, "THE ONLY PLAN"

Your chosen career

_____

College or training required

_____

Other skills or aspects you must sharpen

_____

Is your career choice to broad?   Y / N

_____

Or not broad enough?   Y / N

_____

Is there a realistic number of careers available for you in the environment you want?

Y / N _____

Do you need to save money or find financing?

Y / N _____

Who in your life can help keep you on track for success?

_____

When will you unveil your plans to this person and ask them to help keep you accountable?

_____

CAREER 2 – PLAN B, "THE YOU'RE NOT GOING TO NEED IT, BUT JUST IN CASE PLAN"

Your chosen career

_____

College or training required

_____

Other skills or aspects you must sharpen

_____

Is your career choice to broad?   Y / N

_____

Or not broad enough?   Y / N

_____

Is there a realistic number of careers available for you in the environment you want?

Y / N _____

Do you need to save money or find financing?

Y / N _____

Who in your life can help keep you on track for success?

_____

When will you unveil your plans to this person and ask them to help keep you accountable?

_____

Let the things you have found out about yourself through this guide sink in. Rework your vow, your Ikigai, your Immutable Laws and even redo this guide if it's time for a change. Write down your hobbies on your whiteboard so you can keep yourself busy and carry around your vow card with these goals one by one, update them when you complete them.

People with goals succeed because they know where they are going and can keep themselves on track; plant your goal in your mind. Print this. Carry each individual goal around with you daily and look at it often. Remember, **dreams are just dreaming until we take action**!

VOW/IKIGAI

_____

IMMUTABLE LAWS

_____
_____
_____
_____
_____

Step 1 _____ Time Frame_____

Step 2 _____ Time Frame_____

Step 3 _____ Time Frame_____

Step 4 _____ Time Frame_____

Step 5 _____ Time Frame_____

Step 6 _____ Time Frame_____

Step 7 _____ Time Frame_____

Step 8 _____ Time Frame_____

Step 9 _____ Time Frame_____

Step 10 _____ Time Frame_____

ABOUT THE AUTHOR & ADDITIONAL READING LIST

WWW.PLANNINGADULTING.COM

ABOUT THE AUTHOR:

Don't worry about me! Go on, get out there and get on with your life!

Top: Kyle & Emilee Crandall, Piz Gloria, Schilthorn, Switzerland; Bottom: Kyle's original chart

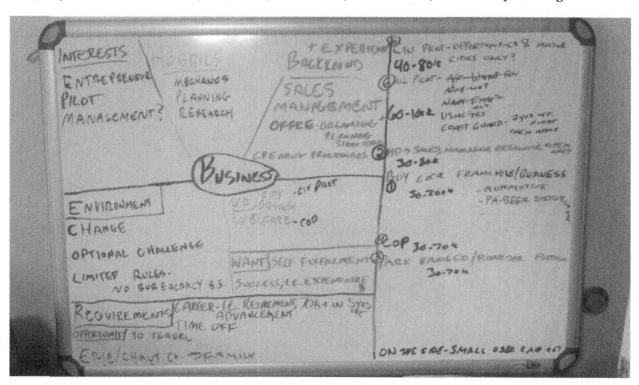

Works cited and resources for further information:

NEED	LOCATION
Business help?	ANY book or presentation by Mike Michalowicz
	Clock Work
	Profit First
	Pumpkin Plan
	Surge
	The Toilet Paper Entrepreneur
	https://www.mikemichalowicz.com
Confidence?	*The Little Green Book of Getting Your Way* by Jeffrey Gitomer
Creativity?	*Thinkertoys* by Michael Michalko
Definitions?	www.Google.com
Hobbies?	www.wikipedia.com
Insight?	Earl Nightingale's – *The Strangest Secret* (on YouTube)
Positivity?	*The Happiness Equation: Want Nothing + Do Anything =*
	Have Everything by Neil Pasricha
Resolve?	*The Undefeated Mind* by Dr. Alex Lickerman

McHorse, Mindy Tyson. "57 Things Other People Want From Life." August 2011. American Writers & Artists Inc. https://www.awai.com/2011/08/57-things-other-people-want-from-life/.

Ganley, Addi. "Monthly Budget" chart. Frugal Fanatic. www.frugalfanatic.com. Accessed 22 Apr.
2019.

Hawks, Dr. Douglas. "The Difference Between Wants vs Needs in Economics." Lesson Transcript Chapter 62 / Lesson 3. "https://study.com/academy/lesson/the-difference-between-wants-vs-needs-in-economics.html"

Robinson, Michael T. Career Planner.com. Career Test & Career Counseling, List of over 12,000 Careers, 2018, https://www.careerplanner.com/ListOfCareers.cfm. Accessed 22 Apr. 2019.

Wikipedia. List of Hobbies, 2019, https://en.wikipedia.org/wiki/List_of_hobbies. Accessed 22 Apr. 2019. "fair use under United States copyright law. Other uses of this image, on Wikipedia or elsewhere, might be copyright infringement." Work is released under CC-BY-SA: http://creativecommons.org/licenses/by-sa/3.0/.

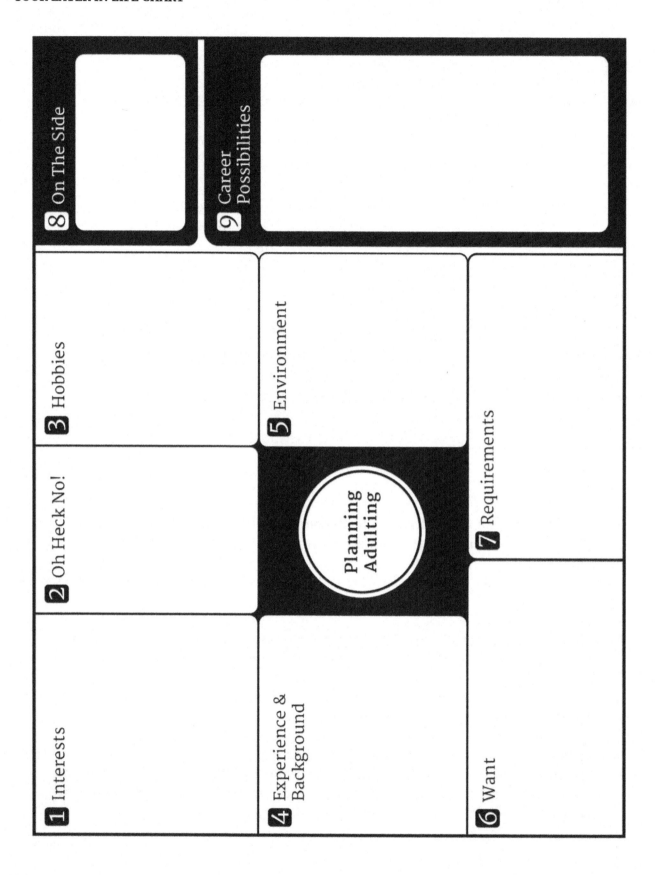

1 Interests

2 Oh Heck No!

3 Hobbies

4 Experience & Background

Planning Adulting

5 Environment

6 Want

7 Requirements

8 On The Side

9 Career Possibilities

If this guide helped you:

Please share the love by sharing these cards!!

And leave me a positive review on Amazon!

Not happy with this experience?

Please contact me, I want to know!

Success@PlanningAdulting.com

PLANNING ADULTING

A MOTIVATIONAL INTERACTIVE WORKBOOK.

Kyle Crandall

success@planningadulting.com
www.planningadulting.com

PLANNING ADULTING

A MOTIVATIONAL INTERACTIVE WORKBOOK.

Kyle Crandall

success@planningadulting.com
www.planningadulting.com

PLANNING ADULTING

A MOTIVATIONAL INTERACTIVE WORKBOOK.

Kyle Crandall

success@planningadulting.com
www.planningadulting.com

Made in the USA
Monee, IL
12 November 2020